Sisterlocking
Discoarse

SUNY series in Feminist Criticism and Theory
edited by Michelle A. Massé

SUNY series, Critical Race Studies in Education
edited by Derrick R. Brooms

Sisterlocking
Discoarse

RACE,
GENDER,
AND THE
TWENTY-
FIRST-
CENTURY
ACADEMY

Valerie Lee

Cover art "Unapologetic" by Angelia Lee. Courtesy of the artist.

Published by STATE UNIVERSITY OF NEW YORK PRESS, Albany

For information, contact STATE UNIVERSITY OF NEW YORK PRESS,
Albany, NY
www.sunypress.edu

Library of Congress Cataloging-in-Publication Data

Names: Lee, Valerie, 1950- author.
Title: Sisterlocking discoarse : race, gender, and the twenty-first-century
    academy / Valerie Lee.
Description: Albany : State University of New York Press, 2021. | Series:
    SUNY series in feminist criticism and theory | Includes bibliograph-
    ical references and index.
Identifiers: LCCN 2021030174 (print) | LCCN 2021030175 (ebook) | ISBN
    9781438485850 (hardcover) | ISBN 9781438485843 (paperback) | ISBN
    9781438485867 (ebook)
Subjects: LCSH: Lee, Valerie, 1950- | African American women in higher
    education. | Education, Higher—Social aspects—United States. |
    African American women college teachers—Biography.
Classification: LCC LC2781.5 .L44 2021 (print) | LCC LC2781.5 (ebook) |
    DDC 378.1/2092 [B]—dc23
LC record available at https://lccn.loc.gov/2021030174
LC ebook record available at https://lccn.loc.gov/2021030175

10 9 8 7 6 5 4 3 2 1

DISCOURSE: a scholar's intellectual conversation

DISCOARSE: an intellectual conversation framed by a scholar with coarse hair and with such hair affecting her presence and promise in academe

For my family who supported my academic career:

To Erica, my first-born, nursed between classes and raised on a college campus

To Jessica who was so enamored by her kindergarten teacher that she quoted this teacher daily. When I reminded her that I, too, was a teacher, she burst out crying, "You're not a teacher. You're a mommy."

To Adam who grew waist-length dreadlocks, and when hearing that I was going to write something about hair automatically heard "discourse" as "discoarse."

To Andrew who was so used to going throughout the neighborhood selling candy, popcorn, and holiday cards for his scouting troop that when one of my books was published asked if I wanted him to take the book house to house to sell.

To James, my personal attorney and husband, the trailing partner to all of my academic events, who after enjoying these events would come home and remind me that the academy is crazy.

And to my mother, Ann, who vicariously lived my career.

Much thanks to my colleagues across many academic departments and academic support units. Were it not for your collegiality and commitment, my career would have been less fulfilling, less joyous.

Although I cannot acknowledge all the students I taught, I do want to give a shout-out to those advisees with whom I shared ideas, life experiences, and watched become professionals in their own right, many while maintaining a bond with each other: Aaron, Alison, Aneil, Antonia, April, Aya, Barbara, Bennis, Brandon, Candace, Candice, Chris, Chiquita, Christiana, Constance Sue, Corrie, Crystal, Danielle, Deborah, Deveonne, Dionne, Donna Jean, Durene, Eleni, Elizabeth, Esther, Gerardina, Indya, Julia, Kaavonia, Kalenda, Karen, Kelly Jo, Lakesia, Leslie, Lindell, Lisa Marie, Lu, Monica, Nancy, Nuzhat, Riggy, Robin, Rosemary, Roxanne, Ruth, Sarah, Shannon, Sheri, Shobanna, Simone, Sonia, Steve, Susan, Tayo, Tiffany, Tim, Tonya, Valora, Vernell, Yoshie, and all those I should have named had I checked my Facebook account.

A special thanks also to all the members of Womanist Readers, my favorite and longest lasting circle of readers. Janet, I could not have sustained a thirty-plus-year reading group without your help. And to my sister, Patty, who has told me that I must acknowledge her in all of my books: thanks for being my traveling companion to the Womanist Readers gatherings and the person with whom I have daily chats.

I want to thank Kimberly Kovarik for her willingness in lending expertise for not just this project but my projects over the span of many years.

Additionally, I am deeply indebted to Cheri Fisher Wilson, executive director of advancement and development at Oakwood University, who when called upon at the last minute to update pictures of a slave cemetery, promptly and graciously responded. Much thanks to Drina Phillip of Phillip's Photography and Videography for the family photograph, and special blessings to educator/designer Angelia Lee, who shared her cartoons, cover design painting, and sisterly friendship.

I gratefully acknowledge those entities that have allowed me to reprint and expand published material. SUNY Press has generously allowed me to reprint for this book three essays that I have revised and expanded: chapter 1: "Sisterlocking Power: Or How Is Leadership Supposed to Look?" in *Black Womanist Leadership: Tracing the Motherline,* ed. Toni C. King and S. Alease Ferguson (2011); chapter 3: "Smarts: A Cautionary Tale" from *Calling Cards: Theory and Practice in the Study of Race, Gender, and Culture,* ed. Jacqueline Jones Royster and Ann Marie Mann Simpkins (2005); and chapter 5: "Pearl Was Shittin' Worms and I Was Supposed to Play Rang-Around-the-Rosie?": An African American Woman's Response to the Politics of Labor" from *Over Ten Million Served: Gendered Service in Language and Literature Workplaces,* ed. Michelle A. Massé and Katie J. Hogan (2010). Chapter 10 includes the essay "Reclaiming, Reframing, and Reimagining Service: A Career in Retrospect," *ADE Bulletin* 157, 2020, published by the Modern Language Association of America.

James Peltz, associate director and editor in chief; Ryan Morris, senior production editor; Michael Sandlin, copyeditor; Rebecca Colesworthy, acquisitions editor; and the entire SUNY editorial team have been the best. (Rebecca, meeting you at the 2019 Chicago Modern Language Association Book Exhibit was like discovering a women's, gender, and sexuality studies colleague I had always wanted to meet. Count us as friends for life!)

Finally, I want to thank my family of faith—brothers and sisters who have nourished my spirit, visited me when sick, and uplifted me when down. Your reward is forthcoming.

Introduction

Themes: Why Begin with Hair?

Miz Valerie, What do you want to do with your new growth?
> —JEANNIE, my hairdresser

What to do with new growth is a choice that over the years many Black women have faced, for it is the hair's new growth that exposes texture untouched by chemicals, hot combs, flat irons, dyes, or anything meant to "relax" the hair. This is a book about new growth. Although its foundational metaphors are taken from Black women's hair politics, it is fundamentally a book about how a young Black woman finishing her doctorate in the late 1970s and retiring forty-some years later as a vice provost and vice president at one of the nation's largest universities learned to navigate an academy that was not quite ready for Brown and Black women. Because I did not look like most of my colleagues, at every stage of my career I literally confronted the issue of what to do with my hair in tandem with how to manage new growth opportunities presented by professional advancements. Like my hair's own new growth, the experiences that I share are not always in a linear sequence but coiled in my memories in different ways. Some of these memories are downright nappy; others reflect straightening processes that I probably needed as I am what higher education now calls a first-generation underrepresented student.

For Black professional women, hair has been a chronological, cultural, and climate thermometer. Chronologically, some of this book's early essays were written when natural hair was not considered professional. When I was graduating from high school, Afros were beginning to come in style, a detail I remember because my predominately white high school had one hair rule: if one's hair flowed downward, it could be as long as one wanted it to be, but any hair spiraling upward had to be within so many inches from the scalp. Of course, the only hairstyles that stood stalwartly upward were the Black students' Afros. During my late teens and early twenties, I had gone through the Afro stage in college, but by grad school, I was back to perms. As of that time, I had not read Gwendolyn Brooks's poem "To Those of My Sisters Who Kept Their Naturals—never to look a hot comb in the teeth." By midcareer, and after having taught many Black women authors who wrote proudly about hair, I became uncomfortable teaching what I was not living. Hair became a cultural thermometer. While teaching Toni Morrison's *Sula* (1976), how could I empathize with Nel's evolving disinterest in hot combs and smooth hair if I was unwilling to listen to the Sula sisterhood in my own life who, too, were championing their natural selves? Or how many times could I teach Morrison's *Song of Solomon* (1997) and hear Hagar's crying awareness that her lover, Milkman, did not love her "soft damp wool"[1] hair without acknowledging my own unease with my permed hair? And how long could I be critical of the characters in Morrison's *Tar Baby* (1993) who saw twisted, locked hair as low class if I had been unwilling to let my own hair challenge professional status norms? Among their many themes, the one theme that every Black woman author that I taught seemed to be addressing was beauty aesthetics, from the "I" voice in Ntozake Shange's *Nappy Edges* (1978) to Celie's voice in Alice Walker's *The Color Purple* (1982), to the two-headed woman's voice in Lucille Clifton's poem, "Homage to My Hair," who declares that her nappy hair "is as tasty on your tongue as good greens / Black man."[2]

As I moved from a professor in the world of my own office and my own classroom to the larger world of academic service across the university, the university's Big Ten Academic Alliance, and the national Association of Departments of English, hair became a climate thermometer because in the early years of administration no one looked like me. I was a professional with braids, an oxymoron. How does one gain authority with what my grandma used to call "plaits," twisted Black Medusa appendages straight out of picka-ninny heads? With orchestrated resistance on the part of several of us sistahs, the academy did change. In fact, as time moved on, my sistah colleagues and

I were able to wear our natural hairstyles long before corporate America welcomed or tolerated our friends to do so. By the time I retired, I was sporting braids every day for the full five-year term as a vice president and vice provost, working alongside an African American dean of student life whose regal looks were framed by blonde-dyed natural hair defiantly cut as short as possible. She is now a college president.

Thus, for professional Black women, hairstyles are literal decisions that affect career choices, as well as a metaphor for claiming one's freedom, defying Anglo-beauty aesthetics, and celebrating organic growth. That a Black woman academic could or would write about hair never occurred to me until I had the occasion to be in an audience of women's studies scholars listening to a young scholar, Noliwe M. Rooks, speak of her forthcoming monograph on hair. I sat there mesmerized and proud that Black women's hair could be a scholarly topic and that a university press was going to publish the work. That manuscript became *Hair Raising: Beauty, Culture, and African American Women* (1996). Rook historicizes African American hair culture through a study of advertisements in periodicals that targeted Black women audiences. Focusing largely on self-made, self-constructed, and self-authored Madame C. J. Walker, who is associated with popularizing the hot comb and building a multimillion-dollar enterprise, *Hair Raising* is the urtext that gave other Black academics the green light to write our own stories about our bodies.

In 2001 another notable text followed: *Hair Story: Untangling the Roots of Black Hair in America* by Ayana D. Byrd and Lori L. Tharps. Whereas *Hair Raising* begins its history of the production and consumption of Black hair products from the mid-1880s to the early 1990s, the historical sweep in *Hair Story* spans from fifteenth-century Africa to America in the new millennium, examining everything from how hairstyles among African cultures revealed clan identities and geographic locations, to the African American mass production of the plastic Afro pick comb, to Americanized dreadlocks, to hair trends adopted by hip-hop trendsetters. The other text arriving as the new millennium dawned was Juliette Harris and Pamela Johnson's edited volume, *Tenderheaded: A Comb-Bending Collection of Hair Stories* (2001). *Tenderheaded* includes sixty essays by a range of writers reclaiming the politics of Black hair by using the metaphors of Black hair styling and sculpting: (e.g., "It All Comes Down to the Kitchen," by Henry Louis Gates Jr.; "The Kink That Winked," by Cynthia Colbert; "Cornrow Calculations (or Math is Beauty)," by Toni Wyn; "Hot Comb" by Natasha Trethewey; "A Happy Nappy Hair-Care Affair" by Linda Jones). Although indebted to those who wrote these histories of and commentaries on Black hair, my emphasis is on journeying through and navigating spaces I was never meant to occupy. In *Sisterlocking Discoarse*, hair is head covering for a book that seeks to do what I did best as a professor: mentor a new generation of thinkers for a more inclusive society. Like skin color, hair for me was always a site of difference. In this book, it is the medium that prompts my thinking on how academic leadership looks, performs, and changes.

Chronology: Why a Text Over So Many Years?

Memory is a queer creature, an eccentric curator.
            —TAYARI JONES, *An American Marriage*

The ideas and words in *Sisterlocking Discoarse* have been circulating in my head and landing on yellow pads and computer keys from 1976 to 2018. Some thoughts became keynote speeches, conference presentations, blogs, and of course, journal articles. Thus, this book is a compilation of essays previously published (and essays never published) that follow my journey through the academy from my early days as an assistant professor through the years of full professorship and senior administration, ending with receiving my discipline's highest service award. I would like to say that I was intentional about the book's span of time, but its span of several decades is due to the way that administration disrupts and changes the direction of scholarly pursuits. The result, however, is that the extended time span has served to affirm as well as complicate the unpacking of my experiences and memories. Over time, memory becomes what Tayari Jones terms an "eccentric curator."[3] My arbitrariness of memory needed just one moment to move from eccentric to common, from personal to communal, and that moment arrived in the summer of 2020.

SUMMER 2020

Today's current racial and gender social justice movements are why this book is unapologetic in its continued emphasis on categories of difference in twenty-first-century America. Although the chapters span experiences from the late 1970s through the early decades of the new millennium, I am writing this preface two years after my final retirement, in summer 2020. Some are already calling this summer "The Lost Summer" because of the COVID-19 virus with its mandate to shelter-in-place, maintain social distance, and self-quarantine.

Airlines are grounded, 401(K) accounts have tanked, many restaurants are closed, millions are unemployed, the best of plans derailed, and well over two hundred thousand Americans have died. It is a time when the prefix "un" is overused, starting with unprecedented, quickly followed by uncharted, unexpected, unfathomable, unjust, unknown, unpredictable, unstoppable, unsurvivable, untimely, and unusual. Most notably, with its disinfecting and distancing protocols, the summer of 2020 is a time in America with not just one but two interconnected public health crises: the COVID-19 virus and the systemic racism virus. As of this writing, neither virus has a cure or a protective vaccine.

Summer 2020 measures time on grand and minute scales: four hundred years of slavery, 150 years postemancipation; and nine minutes and twenty-nine seconds of losing breath—the length of time that a white policeman kneeled on the neck of George Floyd, a Black man who could not breathe, crying for his mama. Thus, from my point of view today, I toyed with going back and doing updates on some of the essays. A prime example of an essay that could be rewritten over and over again is chapter 2, the letter to my sons. First written as a university blog when I was shaken by the death of Eric Garner and later revised after the Trayvon Martin case, I now am writing this preface on the heels of the deaths of Rayshard Brooks, George Floyd, Ahmaud Arbery, Sandra Bland, Breonna Taylor, Michael Brown, Freddie Gray, Tamir Rice, and many others—each name graced with a hashtag. I do not want to keep rewriting that same letter. Every rewrite reopens wounds. Every time a Black mother has to repeat "The Talk" her voice chokes. Years ago when I wrote chapter 2, "We Can't Breathe," I did not know that the literal loss of breath and the metaphorical emphasis on the strangulation of Black and Brown lives would reach a crescendo culminating in protesters world-wide carrying signs saying No Justice, No Peace; White silence is violence; Disarm Hate, and yes, Black Lives Matter. I could not have known that my admonitions to my sons about driving while Black needed to encompass jogging while Black through white neighborhoods, sleeping while Black in one's car at a fast-food drive-through, and birdwatching while Black in a city park. Many of these situations have ended in death for Black men.

In addition to contemplating changes to chapter 2, I toyed with uplifting the tone in chapter 4. As someone who has served as a chief diversity officer, my discussions on diversity and implementing inclusive excellence in chapter 4 are not as hopeful as they might be if I were rewriting them this summer. The smell of change is in the air and caution thrown to the wind in the presence of a pandemic. Racial reckoning demands change: cities and states are rewriting rules for law enforcement; legislators are asking that Juneteenth be declared a federal holiday and that the Black national anthem, "Lift Every Voice and Sing," be sung at national events; corporations are donating funds for implicit bias workshops; activists are toppling the statues representative of the Confederacy; NASCAR is banning the Confederate flag from its racetracks; Mississippi is retiring its long-standing original state flag; after eighty-seven years the Washington Redskins football team is retiring its racist name and logo; the musical group Dixie Chicks is dropping its first name and another musical group, Lady Antebellum, is dropping its last name; the sitcom "The Simpsons" is hiring actors of color to voice characters of color; and Quaker Oats is retiring its mascot, Aunt Jemima.[4]

This last change struck close to home, to the interior of my kitchen table where I enjoyed eating pancakes while collecting the early advertisements of the Aunt Jemima brand. I was literally eating my scholarship. Over the years, I have noted that even after the company reduced the weight of this jolly Black pancake maker, even after taking the kerchief off of her hair, even after adorning her with pearls and lace, it was not enough to shake off stereotypic dust. As with the Confederate statues, Aunt Jemima reeked too much of a bygone era of idyllic plantation paradises. It was only a matter of time for the hip-hop generation to derisively dismiss Aunt Jemima as "yo, mama" and for poet Cheryl Boyce-Taylor to write a poem whose first line asks, "Will the new aunt Jemima have dreads?" ("After Robert Fuller" in Poem-a-Day on July 27, 2020, by the Academy of American Poets).

All of the changes to statutes, monuments, emblems, and icons that are currently in progress complement the point that I made years ago in chapter 9 when describing how out of place I felt when traveling world sites that showcased only Eurocentric images and viewpoints. At the time when I wrote on how conflicted I was strolling the streets, squares, and plazas of Brussels while remembering the history of the Congo, I had not imagined that during the summer of 2020, the sixtieth anniversary of Congolese rule, city employees in Ghent would hoist the bust of Belgium's King Leopold II off its pedestal. When I wrote chapter 9 about visiting plazas around the world, wondering what direction to go to find fragments of Black history, I had not imagined that one day in our nation's capital near the White House itself there would be a place called Black Lives Matter Plaza, located not on the Sixteenth Street NW that I knew, but now on Black Lives Matter Street. Neither did I imagine that structures that always meant much to me would become even more

Figure I.1. Black Lives Matter. Neighbor Lucinda B. Headrick and my grand-children, London and Chase Cochran, on their way to a local rally, Atlanta, Georgia, summer 2020.

powerful icons, such as a bridge in Alabama. Congressman John Lewis, who had crossed the Edmund Pettus Bridge in Selma, Alabama, so many times in life, crossed it one final time in a horse-drawn hearse on Sunday, July 26, 2020.

With so many changes, the air this summer portends that meaningful changes will take place, from eliminating no-knock warrants to criminal-izing the chokehold. It is no accident that the immediate changes focus on the body. As Ta-Nehisi Coates contends, "All our phrasing—race relations, racial chasm, racial justice, racial profiling, white privilege, even white supremacy— serves to obscure that "racism is a visceral experience, . . . it dislodges brains, blocks airways, rips muscle, extracts organs, cracks bones, breaks teeth."[5] The physicality of George Floyd's death awakened viewers worldwide. With this summer's protests there seem to be more vocal allies of social justice from a wider spectrum of races and generations. In this regard, I smile at a pho-tograph of my grandchildren who live in Atlanta on their way to a social justice rally accompanied by their senior white activist neighbor. Although my grandchildren are too young to be fully aware of the politics of the Black

Lives Matter sign that is planted in their front yard, their neighbor, Lucinda Headrick, certainly understands the necessity of continuing the fight for a more perfect union. All are smiling, the photograph capturing the spirit of collaboration and connection that has been building in local neighborhoods and global communities. A sense of structural inequalities seems to be resonating across bodies, beliefs, and borders. Unlike in earlier years, fewer white people are reacting defensively, countering and diluting the Black Lives Matter signs with All Lives Matter. Most notably, it is summer 2020 wherein a presidential candidate on a major ticket has selected a woman of color as his choice for vice president. Incremental and major changes permeate the airwaves, but only time will tell if minds and hearts are truly changing, if there will be measurable outcomes and sustainable solutions. Just like contact tracing is difficult but necessary in controlling the spread of COVID-19, successful contact tracing for the racial virus calls for identifying all those with whom a racist comes into contact—an impossible task unless legislatures, communities, houses of worship, and yes, the academy, work in concert. Will the social justice energy of summer 2020 last, or will it be like summer 1964, Freedom Summer, when courageous work was done to increase Black voter registration, only to have Black voter registration remain a contested issue for many years to come?

I write this preface also during a time when an African American woman, Tarana Burke, has started the #MeToo movement, prompting women around the globe to expose the sexual indiscretions and crimes of men in business, entertainment, and government circles. If I were writing some of the essays today I would have included incidents that I now have vocabularies and allies to help me unpack. In the previously mentioned chapter 4 where I discuss a racial encounter on a plane, I would have added the story of a flight early in my career that shook my confidence as a Black woman professional. When my seatmate, a white male who was the provost at a prestigious northeastern college, learned that I was an assistant professor at an equally prestigious private liberal arts institution, his arm kept brushing against my thigh and then my left breast. I was naïve enough to think that he was simply reacting to close quarters—although I knew better and departed the plane embarrassed and disappointed that I had not voiced my discomfort or done what my college roommate, an experienced subway rider from Harlem, had instructed me to do in such situations—yell out loud and clear, "Why are you touching my boobs?" Women during summer 2020 have not hesitated to speak loudly and clearly, chanting "Say Her Name." At the same time, it is in summer

2020 that we celebrate the passing of an icon, Supreme Court Justice Ruth Bader Ginsburg, a soft-spoken yet powerful voice for women's equality. With Ginsburg's death, we are reminded that no matter how small our frames, our voices can thunder with power and truth.

The lapse of time from writing some of these essays and penning this introduction during Summer 2020 tempts me in other ways. The final chapter on retirement is a celebration of freedom, but the citywide activities that I would have been enjoying, the Science Festival, Arts Festival, Asian Festival, and Blues & Jazz Festival, have all been canceled. I worry that many will mistake what it feels like to be housebound with what retirement must be like. But a stay-at-home mandate with Zoom gatherings is not retirement. Indeed, this summer's sheltering-in experience has made my plea to my husband James that he retire all the more difficult. Because he is an attorney in solo practice, I managed to get him to watch *Judge Judy* with me. But when during the pandemic I began watching Rachael Ray prepare all kinds of dishes, he accused me of mistaking the pandemic's goal of slowing the spread of the virus, a process called "flattening the curve" with what seemed to be my goal, "fattening my curves." Rather than spending every day in the bliss that I describe in chapter 10, I presently go to James's office a few days a week to help out because the pandemic forced him to furlough his small staff. I had always imagined that if I had attended an HBCU (Historically Black College or University), I probably would have elected to become a lawyer because at an HBCU I would have seen Blacks in all occupations. However, it has taken only a few days at James's law practice for me to feel blessed that I chose a career in higher education. As a professor of English, I stare quizzically at legal language that says, "further affiant sayeth naught"; "Now comes James C. Lee, Esq., Attorney for the Defendant, John Doe , and hereby gives notice of his appearance as counsel in the above styled cases." "Sayeth naught"? "Styled cases"? Everything James writes is "pursuant to. . . " Soon I hope to return to full retirement, to the "reality" television courts where even if the law is mostly entertainment, the language is at least clear.

As mentioned, the long incubation period of *Sisterlocking Discoarse* might have warranted some change of details, but I have chosen to let details mirror their historical period. I do want to note, however, that given the publication of *Sisterlocking Discoarse*, there is at least one other book that will need to make some edits in its next edition. Earlier this calendar year I read *Not Even Past*, a history of the Department of English that I once chaired. As a contributor to that text, I certainly anticipated much of its content. Knowing that I had a manuscript that soon was to be published, but not processing that several of the previous chairs had also written memoirs, I would have alerted the authors of *Not Even Past* (2019) that this statement needed amending: "Two people who have served as Chair of the English Department have published memoirs that cover at least part of their careers."[6] With the publication of *Sisterlocking Discoarse*, the number changes to three. Reading *Not Even Past* confirmed for me that the socially active life that I, as a young, naive graduate student suspected the faculty of having, was indeed true (the bromance road trips, the poker games, the drinking, the dancing). But this is not a story of a student who was involved with the department in one way or another for over forty years and is now writing an exposé. I enjoyed every minute of my graduate years, finishing with a 4.0 cumulative grade point average. Yet if I had read *Not Even Past* prior to writing some of my reflections, I might have been tempted to change some details. Instead, my memories remain intact as mine.

Genres: Why Mix Genres?

It is true that my attempts to write in my own voice have
placed me in the center of a snarl of social tensions and
crossed boundaries.
  —PATRICIA J. WILLIAMS, *The Alchemy of Race and Rights*

From the very beginning of my career I felt the need to draw from my own cultural heritage to supplement and enrich what I was learning from other cultures. As a professor of literature, I admired Black creative writers who insisted on creating their own genres: Ntozake Shange clarifying that *For Colored Girls who considered Suicide when the Rainbow is Enuf* was not a play but a choreopoem; Audre Lorde for terming her autobiography a bio-mythology; Octavia Butler for naming her novel *Kindred* a grim fantasy; and others who consciously wrote outside of prescribed formats. Black women scholars, too, have experimented with genres, most notably law scholar Patricia Williams. When *The Alchemy of Race and Rights* was first published in 1991, I immediately appreciated its use of metaphors, stories, and parables as one of the most interesting law books I had read. Contrastingly, when I team-taught the work with a professor of law and a class divided between third-year law students and doctoral students in arts and humanities, I soon noticed that only the latter group of students was as excited about all the genre mixing as I was. The law students (except for those with undergraduate degrees in English) wanted Patricia Williams to get to the point, cite case law, and be done. I enjoyed her narrative process, her intentional meanderings, her anecdotes, her references to the likes of Shakespeare and Ursula Le Guin. Similarly, I marveled at the way critic Ann duCille wrote *Skin Trade* (1996), a volume that moves from national romance stories, to Black Barbie toy theory, to a formal literary discussion of the occult of true Black womanhood, and to anything she chose when thinking of what she calls "discourse and dat course."[7] Perhaps Black women scholars have created their own definition of discourse because they have had to create their own definitions of themselves as explained in Morrison's *Sula*: "Because each had discovered years before that they were neither white nor male, and that all freedom and triumph was forbidden to them, they had set about creating something else to be."[8] Perhaps the creation of genre is linked to the creation of personhood.

A second reason for my deliberate use of various genres is due to the way I was situated in the academy, in interdisciplinary, intersecting, and interlocking ways. As a professor of English, I also held courtesy appointments in women's, gender, and sexuality studies, comparative studies, the Institute for Folklore Studies, the Center for Interdisciplinary Law and Policy Studies, and African American and African studies, serving on dissertation committees, administrative committees, or performing teaching duties for all of them. These were not lines from a curriculum vitae, or mere professional window dressing. Rather, each appointment represented the performance of substantive work when called upon. This wide exposure gave me respect for various kinds of scholarship: literary analyses, feminist studies, critical race studies, ethnography, folklore studies, and Black performance and cultural studies. Thus, in this book I have chosen to include folk stories, scholarly essays, legal cases, invited speeches, family and office photos, cartoons, a travelogue, and a student essay. I work within spheres where hybridity, creolization, liminality, and intersectionality are serious concepts, not easily contained in generic structures.

Not limiting myself to a specific genre represents a freedom that I have earned. I want to share knowledge and tell stories on my own terms, deliberately mixing the formal and the informal, the academic and the popular. My journey covers a range of roles: a graduate student entering a very large doctoral program, a newly minted assistant professor, a senior professor, and a senior administrator who chaired three different departments. But I also include stories that embrace my other identities: a mother of four children, a wife of a Black attorney with his own small law practice, an executive director of a community book club for over thirty years, and a woman of faith active in a local church. I tell stories about selected professional moments that have informed my thinking on race, gender, power, position, and privilege. Although some of the stories are puzzling at best and jarring at worst, this is not a book about overcoming family or community hardships. And although I would love to be able to claim deep southern roots, this is not a story of Black migration from South to North. I grew up in southern Maryland, barely south of the Mason-Dixon line, sixty miles to be exact. This is not a story of growing up in an impoverished urban 'hood amid generational poverty. Growing up, I never looked poverty in the face until I became a graduate student receiving a tuition benefit and living on a stipend—not generational poverty, but genteel poverty, mere dollars away from having a professional job. Although my brother, sister, and I were raised in a house with one bath-room, one wall of the house was decorated with expensive z-brick and that house sat on over five hundred acres owned by my grandmother's people. Today that country road still carries her maiden name. At sixteen years old I awakened to the fact that the families of my white classmates at the newly integrated high school owned businesses on their land. In adulthood when I returned to visit my grandmother and saw how developers had purchased her family's land for pennies, I knew that there would be little intergenerational transfer of wealth. But by the Black standards of my childhood days, I was middle class. It was not until I sent my own children to a historically Black college that I truly became aware that there were some Black families who were more middle class than mine. My children had the humbling opportu-nity to meet Black bourgies.

In addition to the lack of poverty, blessedly, I cannot lay claim to a story where several of my playmates ended up shot or on death row, although these are valuable stories. Nor is this a story of academic failures—failed tenure bids, failed promotions—although these are also stories that are needed and have meant much to me. Rather, my stories trace a career of a fairly middle-class Black woman who had high grades and ACT scores, performed top-of-the-class college and graduate schoolwork, and earned career advancement opportunities. Nevertheless, I lived a racialized and gendered life where microaggressions were pervasive. Excellence in high school did not protect me from the racial rioting after basketball games when my Black male friends were carted off to jail and their white teammates freed. Nor was I protected from the white high school system that refused to name a Black valedictorian.

Excellent teaching skills did not protect me from students who claimed that their prep-school teachers said they were good writers, so how dare I, a representative from a Black vernacular tradition—one syllable away from Ebonics speech—give them "C" grades on their compositions?

Sisterlocking Discoarse is a work of reflections. It is my parting message to the academy and a thank-you note to all the students who made my career joyous, challenging, and memorable. As Teresa De Lauretis explains in her introduction to *Alice Doesn't*, I too "will tell some stories and retell others. . . . And time and time again the same concerns, issues, and themes will return throughout the essays, each time diffracted by a different textual prism, seen through a critical lens with variable focus."[9] I am deliberate in my blending of scholarship and storytelling, reliving the warmth of a well-taught, interactive graduate seminar.

Chapter 1, "Sisterlocking Discoarse: Or How Is Leadership *Supposed* to Look?" sets the backdrop for my coming to consciousness about hair and the role it would play in my assuming leadership positions. I start with women in my family and their views that often were in contrast to the literature I was reading by African American women writers. The chapter's compilation of autobiography, literary sources and allusions, and diversity "aha" moments establish a pattern for upcoming chapters.

It is hard focusing only on the academic when one is a mother of four children. Family life intervenes and affects how one views events on one's work calendar. Chapter 2 demonstrates the type of intervention that brought theatrical performances of race too close to home. I wrote chapter 2, "When We Can't Breathe: Generational Spirit-Murder" in 2003 after watching *Sleep Deprivation Chamber*, a play cowritten by playwright Adrienne Kennedy and her son, Adam. Chapter 2 shares the original letter that I wrote to my twin sons, Adam and Andrew, when they were months away from turning eighteen years old. Although their father and I had given them "The Talk" (how race in America works) in bits and pieces from the time they entered a predominately white elementary school, my letter was the first time that I shared "the Talk" at length in writing. *Sleep Deprivation Chamber* ends with a young Black man crying to police officers that he can't breathe. At the time that I saw the play and wrote my sons, I could not have known that "I can't breathe" would become the recurring refrain for future Black men's conflicts with police injustice. A little over a decade later, Eric Garner's last gasp was "I can't breathe." I updated my letter to my sons, this time aware that I was writing the letter for public consumption but unaware that there would still be a need for such a letter in 2020 when George Floyd's "I-can't-breathe" cry would reverberate worldwide.

With chapter 3, I am back on track with my professorial posture. "Smarts: A Cautionary Tale" is my commentary on coming of age in the academy. First given as the required inaugural lecture upon promotion to full professorship, I start off doing the expected job of summarizing my previous scholarship and methodologies. Then I seize the moment, not to thank the academy for accepting me in its hallowed halls but to question the way higher education has defined what constitutes intellect, rigor, appropriate subject matter, and methodologies. Who determines smarts? I argue that African American literature and folklore have always questioned what constitutes true education.

Whereas chapter 3 focuses on the scholarly role of professors, chapter 4 focuses on how teaching and diversity converged in my career. Stories of my teaching experiences could fill volumes: comments from students who had never been taught by a Black teacher; ideological conflicts in multicultural classrooms where I was expected to take sides; teacher/student authority issues; canonical debates. "On Learning that I Was Teaching 'N----r Literature'" signals that this is a chapter where I share experiences that jolted me, preparing me to analyze more deeply why so much diversity work is window dressing instead of dressing for success.

Chapter 5, "Pearl Was Shittin' Worms and I Was Supposed to Play Rang-Around-the-Rosie?" turns to the third leg of university performance: service as reflected by the chapter's subtitle, "An African American Woman's Response to the Politics of Labor." By the time I wrote this chapter, I was chairing one of the country's largest English departments, had already chaired a women's studies department, and served on scores of committees on the college, university, and national levels. This chapter confronts the difficult situation that many faculty of color face: the burden and blessing of extraordinary service. Tellingly, even as I was typing the pages to this book manuscript, I sometimes mistakenly typed *sisterworking* instead of *sisterlocking*. Service in the academy is both rewarding and vexed.

Chapter 6, "Underground Railroads on Postracial Tracks" is a shout-out to my literary training. Long before the publication of Toni Morrison's *Beloved*, I was teaching neo-slave narratives and watching how quickly that canon was growing. Neo-slave narratives are a genre that Black writers have refused to let die, long after the legal ending of American slavery. Its many authors include Octavia Butler, J. California Cooper, Michelle Cliff, Charles

Johnson, Gayl Jones, Dolen Perkins-Valdez, Ishmael Reed, Margaret Walker, Colson Whitehead, Sherley Anne Williams, and others. Chapter 6 adds to the scholarship on the subject by connecting the continued presence of slave narratives as a genre to critical race studies and critical Black feminist framings. The chapter focuses on Williams's *Dessa Rose*, Morrison's *Beloved*, and Butler's *Kindred*.

Noting how many of the neo-slave narratives had origins in legal cases, I became interested in how enslaved Black women navigated the judicial system. Hence chapter 7, "Forty Devils Can't Make Me Obey You," describes legal cases by enslaved Black women that I was researching at the same time as taking one of my daughters to college. In my mind the sassiness of the enslaved women and my daughters' eagerness to experience life at a southern, historically Black college connected in surprising ways.

Chapter 8 on cartoons returns to my administrative duties. The chapter describes the cartoons in my desk drawer that I surreptitiously looked at to keep moving on my academic journey. Located primarily in the pages of the *New Yorker* and the *Chronicle of Higher Education*, these cartoons helped me maintain a sense of humor and balance while juggling so many roles. I read the cartoons through a Black feminist, multicultural lens, sometimes identifying with persons or animals that seemed a caricature of my lived experience. As Rebecca Wanzo expresses in *The Content of Our Caricature: African American Comic Art and Political Belonging* (2020), "I feel as if caricature is waiting around the corner, the thing that I may move into or that may overtake me. Sometimes it is an identity that I willfully move into—righteously, vengefully—often because I have become undone by microaggressions."[10] For someone who rarely read the comics while growing up, I began to yearn for comics to relax life's tensions, always wondering if there were comics about Black women. Thus, the chapter ends with a turn toward comics by and about Black women.

After the comedic release, the book returns to a more reflective posture in chapter 9 by defining the person that I have become, someone who realizes that even her life's global travels and international relationships have been raced and gendered. "From Soweto to Harlem, From the Antilles to Accra" chronicles how cultural baggage intervened in fully enjoying my travels throughout Great Britain, Europe, Africa, and the Caribbean. Long before I traveled to different American cities, I traveled internationally. The first time I flew on a plane was when I was nineteen years old, flying from New York to Paris. I saw palm trees in Florence, Italy, before I ever saw them in Miami, Florida;

I saw Switzerland's Matterhorn before seeing Tennessee's Smoky Mountains, and the Seine River before seeing the Mississippi. Somewhere between those early trips and my later years of traveling, I became fixated on landmarks and histories through the eyes of a daughter of the African diaspora.

With chapter 10, *Sisterlocking Discoarse* ends with the comfort of retirement and an epilogue that is a final salute to my grandmother whose words began my opening story. I thought about writing a formal conclusion for those readers who would want a list of action steps for diversifying academia. I certainly have the background to do so and have been a part of many teams that have formulated such lists for various institutions, as well as for specific academic departments.[11] But there are many handbooks on the market and readily available scholarly works on diversity that detail how to formulate a diversity strategic action plan, measure results, and ensure accountability. Although in some of my chapters I inevitably address these issues, for this project I am not as much interested in the prose of diversity and its mechanics as I am its poetry—the thoughts and lived experiences of a woman of color. Because I have settled within me that this will be the last monograph I write, I do not want space to be given to charts, tables, and statistics. I notice that when some people have come to terms with the arc of their lives or when they are gravely ill, their ability to render the poetic rises. In Randy Pausch's *The Last Lecture* (2008), the lecture he gives is not narrowly tailored to his field of computer science but rather "a summation of everything Randy had come to believe."[12] Similarly, when the young neurosurgeon Paul Kalanithi was dying of stage-four lung cancer, he wrote *When Breath Becomes Air* (2016) with a beauty and lyricism that transcends medical record reports. Although my admiration of these works does not stem from any sense of impending mortality, I admire that Pausch and Kalanithi chose to write outside of disciplinary and formalized structures. The task for me became: "What do I want to say about race and gender if my life depended upon it?" I would want an honest narrative that had heart.

Watching Lin-Manuel Miranda's play *Hamilton* with its emphasis on "who lives, who dies, who tells your story" affirmed for me that I wanted to tell my own story on my own terms, a story made more important because as a senior administrator, I literally sat "in rooms where it happened."[13] In sum, *Sisterlocking Discoarse* is about braiding and breathing and believing that a Black woman's journey through the academy is important.

Sisterlocking Discoarse

OR HOW IS LEADERSHIP *SUPPOSED* TO LOOK?

What can we say then about the representation of the Black female body as we begin the twenty-first century? Perhaps simply that history repeats itself given that this body remains a highly contested site of meaning both within and without the Black community and that African American women still struggle with its representation, vacillating between the poles of sentimental normalization and the flaunting of eccentricity. —CARLA L. PETERSON, "Eccentric Bodies"

Without organized struggles like the ones that happened in the 1960s and early 1970s, individual Black women must struggle alone to acquire the critical consciousness that would enable us to examine issues of race and beauty, our personal choices, from a political standpoint.—bell hooks, "Straightening Our Hair"

I chaired three different departments at my university: the departments of English, women's studies, and African American and African studies. My university exhausted all my identities. I have served also as a vice provost of diversity and inclusion while also serving as a vice president of outreach and engagement. Before taking on these senior leadership roles, I was well aware that as an African American woman on a predominately white campus, I did not look like past and present leaders. But I cannot tell my story without first telling the story of my grandmother, Ma Bell.

"Why do colored people always have to disfigure themselves?" At the height of the civil rights movement, this is the question that my grandmother, Lydia Sardonia Morris Bell, asked her Afro-sporting, dashiki-wearing grandchildren. Lydia, or Ma Bell, as everyone in the community called her, had been a beauty in her heyday, a heyday that described beauty as light skinned with "good hair" (long, silky tresses). She was quick to say that some of her "yellow had been wasted"[1] from having married two very black-skinned men. Her recessive genes produced only one light-skinned child and no children who carried forth the purported blue and green eyes of some of her other relatives. Nevertheless, she was very proud of her three daughters and especially her seven sons. She claimed that she also had a set of twin sons who died in infancy, but no one in the family has been able to verify that tale. When my mother confronted my great-grandma, Annie Mason, about Ma Bell's claim of having birthed twins, her reply was "the devil is going to cut out that gal's tongue for lying." Annie, who was born a few years after slavery ended and whose own mother supposedly had seven sons "sold from the Carolinas to Florida," never confirmed the existence of Ma Bell's twins.

By the time I came along, Ma Bell's first grandchild and only four years younger than her last child, my Uncle Brooke, Ma Bell was stoop-shouldered with very few years left—or so we thought. Although we grandchildren loved to run to her house for her chicken-and-rice dishes, we were well aware that if our behavior got out of hand, she would not hesitate to pin us against a wall or pinch us tightly. Although she had only an eighth-grade education, Ma Bell had worked in some of the richest homes in Greenwich, Connecticut, and knew all about world affairs, as well as having the self-proclaimed dubious ability "to set a table with so much silverware that poor, ignorant white folks back in southern Maryland won't know which fork to use."

She had lived long enough to watch "colored people" go through all kinds of changes. I remember the day that a distant cousin, Freddie, corrected the terms that she was using:

"Colored people," Freddie interrupted her tirade, "we're not colored anymore, Ma Bell."

"Colored people, Negroes, Blacks, whatever y'all are calling yourselves now," grandmother retorted.

It was not that Grandma worshipped white people. She did not. In fact, she could not stand most of them. She had worked in the homes of too many upper-class folks from as far south as Baltimore, Maryland, to as far north as

Greenwich, Connecticut, to think that race was a determinate of manners, or intelligence, or anything that really mattered. Ma Bell never doted over white children or held her lip when sassin' white employers. And she was quite protective of her race when whites criticized Blacks in her presence. During Nixon's presidency, one of her employers expressed joy that Nixon had taken crime off the streets of Washington, DC. My grandmother's swift reply was, "He took it off the streets and placed it in the White House."

A very smart woman, Ma Bell was especially protective whenever anyone hinted that her children or grandchildren were not intelligent. From the time I was very young, she was quite proud of how well I could read. Once, when I was around eight years old, I went to visit her in one of those Greenwich, Connecticut mansions where she worked as cook, maid, nanny, or whatever was needed. (Of course, this meant that her ten children were in Maryland without a mother because out of necessity she had to mammy someone else.) Grandma overheard me arguing with a little white girl who was the same age as I was. We both wanted to read the story and were fighting over the opportunity to do so. In a whirlwind, Grandma raced into the room, grabbed the book from the white girl, and announced, "My granddaughter can read." I felt vindicated. Slaves may not have learned how to read, but her granddaughter knew how to read and read well. And I was just as proud of my grandmother's explanation when fourteen years later at my graduation from a private college in New England, a white woman asked her to explain the foreign words (*magna cum laude*) attached to my name. Unable to read Latin, but knowing that I had studied abroad in France, Grandma used her sharp wit to quickly formulate a response: "When you have traveled, your name must reflect all the places where you have been." She was proud that I planned to continue traveling and reaching more academic milestones, as long as I did not "educate myself pass God"—her way of saying do not lose your beliefs, faith, and humility.

I grew up watching my grandmother assume all kinds of leadership roles. Her style was to do what was needed to get the job done. When we got on her nerves, she would take her five-foot, one-inch frame and swing us against the walls or shake us silly. Today, she would be arrested for child abuse. Back then, she raised grandchildren, neighborhood children, and foster children, and we all loved the many birthday parties she hosted for us, the freedoms she gave to us that only grandparents know how to give, and the open house that she kept. She hated going to senior citizen classes because old people bored her.

Instead, she enjoyed young people, eventually embracing all the identity and racial politics changes that we were expounding.

As with so many African American women, Ma Bell used the moments while braiding hair to dispense her wisdom. As the narrator states in *Dessa Rose*, Sherley Anne Williams's neo-slave narrative, "Child learn a lot of things setting between some grown person's legs, listening at grown peoples speak over they heads."[2] Ma Bell, who lived through perms, Afros, Jheri curls, hair extensions, and synthetic and human hair braids, never missed a moment using hair as a site of political struggle. When she lost most of her hair, she refused to wear a wig, declaring that "you are what you are, and this is what I am. Besides it's not what's on your head; it's what's in it."

When Ma Bell was in her eighties and nineties, her arthritic fingers prevented her from braiding the hair of her great-grandchildren. She no longer had a captive audience to tell her tales of how she had set people and the world straight. On trips home, I tried to explain to her what I did in my new role as a departmental chair. She concluded that I wasn't teaching—I was running the whole university. As someone who had worked several jobs all of her life, she was not surprised by the long hours that I labored; she never expected me to stay home, even after I gave birth to twins and had four children under the age of four. She worked, my mother worked, I worked. My one regret is that by the time I had finished moving into my women's studies office, she was ninety-nine years old and too weak to travel to visit me. Had she been able to visit, she probably would have made a comment about my office décor, a comment that I would translate a commodification of Africanness: Haitian and Jamaican sculpture on the bookshelves; a copper figurine of five women of color holding hands with the inscription "Feminist Five"; several brightly colored Varnette Honeywood paintings; and a sculpture of a Brown woman wearing a headscarf. All of these items would follow me to my final university office where I added other diversity décor: ceramic plaques featuring Toni Morrison's novels; a flower made from pop cans by women with disabilities; posters from the Harlem Renaissance, an oblong Native American multicolored rainmaker stick filled with tiny pebbles, and all kinds of ethnic odds- and-ends. As figures 1.1 and 1.2 ("Black Offices Matter") demonstrate, my office was a place that invited Afrocentric dress styles.

The presence of these ethnic figurines, pictures, and artifacts occasioned one visitor to my office to ask, "How do you think this office will make white

Figure 1.1 and Figure 1.2. Black Offices Matter. Proudly posing in my Diversity and Inclusion office in Hale Hall on the campus of Ohio State University. Note all the ethnic artifacts in the background. March 4, 2015.

students feel when they come to have a conference with you?" My first impulse was to assure the visitor that I had standard items in the office, too. Due to the recycling of old furniture, I ended up with the furniture that had once been in astronaut John Glenn's office. And certainly, the chairs, conference table, and elliptical exercise machine (that I never used) were all the products made by white companies. In fact, my final office was housed in a building that used to be the first student union on a public university campus, which explains why perpendicular to the spider plant in figure 1.2, but unseen in the photograph, is a dumbwaiter that brought food from the ground floor to my office floor. When I did not readily respond to my visitor's question, she asked again, "How do you think this office will make white students feel when they come to have a conference with you?" No one asks Black students how the offices of white faculty make them feel. Because whiteness typically is an unmarked racial category, the offices of white faculty are seen as the norm, their decorating habits neutral, so anything different risks being judged as poor professional taste. Audiences are assumed to be white. As Toni Morrison says in her preface to *Playing in the Dark*, "Until very recently, and regardless of the race of the author, the readers of virtually all of American fiction have been positioned as white."[3] Rather than giving my visitor a full-scale lecture, I shared with her another historical gem about the building that housed my office. As a plaque outside the building indicates, the site once served as a stop on the Underground Railroad.

A few months after Ma Bell died, I ended my first year as chair of the Department of Women's Studies. The editor of the department's newsletter asked me for the obligatory column on what I had learned about administration. What I had learned, however, had nothing to do with the fundamentals of management. My learning had its own set of Murphy's Laws: on the one morning when you decide not to read the fifty new email messages, the provost, trustees, and state legislators will change the location of the 7:30 a.m. power-breakfast meeting; on the one college survey that you decide to complete the night before it is due, question fifteen will ask you for information that you needed to have begun compiling ten days earlier; on the one day that your fiscal officer is on vacation, the dean will ask you a complicated question about the budget. So, I was still too caught up in the minutiae of all the paperwork on my desk to write a column that aspired to heights higher than the stack of memoranda in my inbox.

As an alternative, my editor asked if I would do a typical "state-of-the-department" address. Well, my department was an excellent one, and I could have easily written this type of message. However, having recently attended my daughter's high school graduation and the graduations of eight of my friends' children, I did not want to hear another word about "success," "dreams," or "achievement." Rather, I chose to write a column about what made me most apprehensive about assuming the position of a departmental chair: hair politics.

That's right. Hair politics. But not just any type of hair politics—African American women's hair politics. The Ma Bell arguing-with-her-children type of hair politics. The type of hair politics that Audre Lorde questions in her article, "Is Your Hair Still Political?" and Alice Walker exposes in her essay, "Oppressed Hair Puts a Ceiling on the Brain." I had spent a considerable amount of my personal time during my first year as chair thinking about the type of hair that Toni Morrison describes in *Tar Baby* as "wild, aggressive, vicious hair that needed to be put in jail. Uncivilized, reform-school hair. Mau Mau. Attica, chain-gang hair."[4] Just when I reached the point in my career when I wanted to "go natural" (because full professors can go anywhere they want), I was asked to make a rather conservative move—become a departmental chair.

In workshops for new chairs, there are sessions on tenure and promotion, on what to do when there is money in the budget and what to do when there is a deficit. There are workshops on how to handle difficult colleagues, write annual review letters, job appointment letters, promotion and tenure letters, thank-you-to-donor letters—everything except how to wear one's hair in the natural styles available to Black women and still look "professional." Obviously, African American women aren't the ones running the faculty training workshops at most research-intensive universities. Otherwise, gender and racial representation of leadership would be on the agendas. I first became a department chair in the 1990s, well before there were that many African American women professors in departments and certainly long before most of them advanced to full professor status and began competing for chair positions.

As a full professor, especially one in women's studies, I could have sat in my office and shaved, spiked, purpled, or done anything I wanted to my hair. Among our undergraduate and graduate students, nothing I could have done with my hair would have seemed odd. But as a *chair*, I had to go out and greet people who still thought Afros were radical or the new wave of Black teens wearing bantu knot, cornrow, and sisterlock[5] hairstyles too ethnic. How would I look in what sistahs call "sisterlocks," but what many outside African American communities, and even some within, call "dreadlocks"? The difference between the two words is the difference between affection and fear. Reportedly, the term *dreadlocks* came about when Europeans first encountered Africans' hair in locked styles. They saw the hair as "dreadful." It would be only a matter of years before Blacks would reclaim the term.

Just when I was prepared to go cold turkey with my plan (the first step in locking relaxed or processed hair is to cut off all your hair), I had to come up with an alternative that would not be as shocking. As a new departmental chair, I had to revert to a longer, more gradual plan of growing and cutting and braiding and unbraiding. I know that some people noticed that I had at least five major hairstyle changes that first year and wanted to know why but were too polite to ask. Here is the answer: everything was in preparation for locking, a style that at the time was thought to be more fitting for the Ziggy Marleys and Lauryn Hills of the world than those who wield academic power. Although Alice Walker and Toni Morrison proudly wore dreadlocks, they were not department chairs. The decision I most debated was which type of locks/locs I wanted: combed twists, two-stranded twists, Nubian locks, silky locks, genie locks, extension locks, sisterlocks. One can check out the full photo gallery on many online sites.

In women's studies, we discuss issues relating to body politics. Certainly, in Black women's studies the body has always been a contested site. Whole categories of Black women have been dismissed, derided, and devalued based on their bodies. When conducting research on the dwindling numbers of Black lay midwives who delivered a nation of babies during the first decades of the twentieth century, I discovered that one of the ways that health officials discredited them was through their physical appearance and their bodily parts. They were told that their hands that had "caught" so many babies were too "fleshy" and unclean. When County Health Boards aggressively began to intervene in the lives of Black lay midwives, they began by attacking their bodies. Many started to treat them "as if the grannies were Black [Pontius] Pilates, continually trying to wash off historical prejudices which had already been inscribed on their bodies."[6] In addition to the bodies of Black lay midwives, the bodies of Black mothers themselves have been the subject of much critique. In *Killing the Black Body*, Dorothy Roberts addresses the government's assault on the reproductive rights of Black women. Again, it is a battle that takes place on the bodies of Black women: "White childbearing is generally thought to be a beneficial activity: it brings personal joy and allows the nation to flourish. Black reproduction, on the other hand, is treated as a form of *degeneracy*."[7] In "Wearing Your Race Wrong: Hair, Drama, and a Politics of Representation for African American Women at Play on a Battlefield," Noliwe Rooks refers to the Black female body as a battlefield where "the meaning of certain styles on a Black female body come into conflict with individual understandings held by members of an outside group invested with the power and authority to bring those bodies and styles in line with what they believe to be acceptable."[8]

Although issues of class[9] very much inform the selection of hairstyles, neither vocational nor socioeconomic class have made a marked difference in the ways in which Black women's bodies have been dismissed. Black women who hold professional leadership roles have not escaped society's tendency to critique Black women's bodies and hair technologies.[10] In 1980, Dorothy Reed, a television news reporter, was suspended by the station for wearing cornrows to work. KGO-TV argued the hairstyle was not "consistent" with the station's image.[11] The editors of *Hair Story: Untangling the Roots of Black Hair in America*, in chronicling the recent backlash on Black hairstyles that are read by society as too natural or too nappy, point out that "while corporate America accepts yarmulkes, turbans, and other ethnic or religious signifiers, dreadlocks and other Black hairstyles are often seen as signs of militance and anger."[12] African American women in particular, as literary and cultural critic Ann duCille points out, "By virtue of our race and gender . . . are not only the second sex—the other, in postmodern parlance—but also the last race, the most oppressed, the most marginalized, the most deviant, the quintessential site of difference . . . function[ing] as an erotic icon in the racial and sexual ideology of western civilization."[13]

In response to my grandmother who wondered why Black people would want to "disfigure themselves," the critic in me would answer that Black women are always already disfigured. From the time we first appeared on auction blocks in America, stripped to the waist and deeply probed, we have been reclaiming our bodily rights. In her introduction to *Recovering the Black Female Body*, Carla Peterson speaks of the ways in which Black women have actively responded to bodily assaults and embraced the "eccentricity"[14] "acknowledge[ing] and honor[ing] the eccentric Black female body." Since the 1990s, many Black women professionals are choosing natural hairstyles at the risk of their careers. Defending Black women's right to wear braided hairstyles in the workplace has been the subject of legal cases.

As a mother of two daughters and twin sons, I wanted my children to live during times when their hair was not enslaved by white definitions of professionalism. Although enjoying some of that freedom, my daughters are in occupations where that still is not totally possible without incurring major risks, such as unemployment. Unsurprisingly, my sons have gained such

Figure 1.3. Professional Posture. My son Adam with well-groomed locs, November 2016.

Figure 1.4. "Got Dreads?" Adam wearing "Got dreads?" workout shirt, October 4, 2019.

freedom first, and the one pictured here, Adam, has proudly worn his locs at four different Fortune 500 companies. With a church in the background and not a prison, figure 1.3 seems to be saying that I am a Black man with locs; I am not locked up or in a lockdown situation. I can assume a very formal, professional posture if I so choose. Figure 1.4 is a celebration of life and locs. The upsweep style is perfect for a day of relaxation. The question on the T-shirt "Got dreads?" flips the script. Mimicking the "Got milk?" ads, "Got dreads?" as a logo is actually asking the viewer, "What? Surely, you, too, have dreads." Figure 1.5, "Freedom Locs," demonstrates how, on one head, all the locs are different lengths, with different levels of thickness and curl patterns. It is as

Figure 1.5.
Freedom Locs.
Adam demon-
strating the free
spirit of locs,
May 22, 2019.

if each strand of hair is speaking to the multiplicity of experiences as a Black man, a free Black man.

If Ma Bell were still alive, I would want her to know that my preoccupation with hair and leadership has little to do with hair itself. Rather, it is about agency and whose standards dare announce themselves as definitive in determining the technologies and economies of administrative arenas. Who defines professionalism and how it looks? If Ma Bell were still alive, she would rub her balding head and commend me for bringing to the academy the experiences of Black women, their hair, and their leadership—experiences braided and coiled in the textures, the coarseness of Black hair, of sisterlocking power.

When We Can't Breathe

GENERATIONAL SPIRIT-MURDER

May 9, 2003

To my seventeen-year-old twin sons, Adam and Andrew:

I must now write you a letter that I thought could wait a few months until your eighteenth birthday. The occasion that precipitates this change in timing is last night's performance of Adam and Adrienne Kennedy's *Sleep Deprivation Chamber*. Performed upon the occasion of award-winning playwright Adrienne Kennedy's fiftieth graduation anniversary from Ohio State University, the semiautobiographical play tells the story of a young African American man, Teddy, who while driving home has a confrontation with the police that ends in a brutal beating. The play is based upon a real occurrence that happened to Adam, Adrienne's son. In the play Adam's alter ego is Teddy, and Adrienne's alter ego is Suzanne. Policeman Holzer follows Adam and confronts him in Adam's driveway and then brutally beats him for having a faulty taillight.

I thought for sure that my twenty-five years of teaching African American literature would shield me from an overly emotional response to the play. Certainly, I was equipped to respond as a professor, theorist, and literary critic. But the proximity of my seat a few feet from the violent action of the play and the director's choice to provide a backdrop of animated digital visuals of police brutality in African American communities (as well as pictures of

Emmett Till), force me to respond in the same way as Suzanne, Teddy's educated mother, responds: by letter writing.

Suzanne writes that "our son [Teddy] is being persecuted by the Arlington Police Department just as surely as happened in the Deep South in the 1930s or during Emmett Till's time."[1] I began thinking about Emmett. Emmett's narrative somehow manages to disrupt, intervene in, and assert itself upon so much of African American literature. When white men killed fourteen-year-old Emmett Till for speaking to the woman, for "recklessly eyeballing"[2] a white woman in 1955, African American men were left with mutilated, castrated dreams and African American women with the moan: "Look what they did to my boy."[3] Our narratives have not forgotten Emmett. Works that go back as far as Claude Brown's *Manchild in the Promised Land* (1965) and James Baldwin's *No Name in the Street* (1972), and works as recent as Joan Morgan's *When Chickenheads Come Home to Roost: A Hip-Hop Feminist Breaks It Down* (1999) and Tayari Jones's *Leaving Atlanta* (2002) keep Emmett in our collective unconscious. Long before Emmett appeared on the screen in the play's backdrop, I was already recalling the incident in Toni Morrison's *Song of Solomon* (1977) when Railroad Tommy, Guitar, and Milkman are in a barbershop and hear the news about Emmett. They argue over the (im)possibility of expressing manhood in oppressive situations:

"What the fuck is the difference?" shouted Guitar. "A kid is stomped and you standin round fussin about whether some cracker put it in the paper. He stomped, ain't he? Dead, ain't he? Cause he whistled at some Scarlett O'Hara cunt."

"What'd he do it for?" asked Freddie. "He knew he was in Mississippi. What he think that was? Tom Sawyer Land?"

"So he whistled! So what!" Guitar was steaming. "He supposed to die for that?"

"He from the North," said Freddie. "Acting big down in Bilbo country. Who the hell he think he is?"

"Thought he was a man, that's what," said Railroad Tommy.

"Well, he thought wrong," Freddie said. "Ain't no black men in Bilbo country."[4]

Song of Solomon emphasizes the danger of Black boys who mistake America for "Tom Sawyer Land" and who think that notions of manhood and masculinity are somehow separate from landscape and racial codes. In

Bebe Moore Campbell's *Your Blues Ain't Like Mine* (1992), characters understand that it is part of a white paternalistic code to kill young Black boys and men and that Black boys and men can be "handed over to white men like garbage wrapped in newspaper."[5] Delta codes do not require justice.

However, it is not only our fiction writers who remind us of the fragile existence of young Black boys. Our poets, too, lament the many Emmetts in our history. In Gwendolyn Brooks's "The Last Quatrain of the Ballad of Emmett Till," she writes an archetypal American ballad with blood, dark villains, and empty promises of happiness ever after. There is something about Teddy's story that, like Emmett's story, is

> The last bleak news of the ballad.
> The rest of the rugged music.
> The last quatrain.[6]

My sons, I want you to know that there are reasons why our creative writers and essayists have not let Emmett die. That Adam and Adrienne Kennedy give us a Teddy who can conjure up an Emmett should not come as a surprise. We are never far from Money, Mississippi, never far from the Tallahatchie River, never far from imagining how a seventy-five-pound cotton gin fan can be barb-wired around a young boy's neck, never far from hearing a whistle as a sonic boom. *Sleep Deprivation Chamber* is about what can happen to any young Black boy and the toll his mother pays. But I do not want to make Suzanne's mistake. As Teddy's mother, Suzanne had thought that her middle-class status would protect Teddy. After all, Teddy's mother is a writer, his father a PhD, his uncle a professor emeritus at Stanford, and his sister a Stanford lecturer. Moreover, if the degrees and prestigious schools do not accord enough status, it must be remembered that Teddy's beating takes place in his own driveway, his middle-class yard. He has not left his place or his space. He is on territory that he knows is his father's front yard.

How is it that Suzanne could have thought that middle-class status, her reading of Thoreau and Emerson, would have protected her son? She writes: "I've been to Concord and read Thoreau and Emerson and my grandmother went to church twice a week and our family has worked hard for justice."[7] Perhaps Suzanne had forgotten that African American folklore is replete with jokes that undermine middle-class status: *What do people in Mississippi call a Black man with a PhD? The N-word.* These folk jokes have been crafted from the reality of everyday experiences. In *Race Matters*, Cornel West relates a story about when he was driving from New York to Williams College. Stopped on fake charges of trafficking cocaine, he gives the officer a snapshot of who he really is: "When I told the police officer I was a professor of religion, he replied "Yeh, and I'm the Flying Nun. Let's go nigger!" [8] To the cop, West's PhD in philosophy was just a respelling of the N-word.

Perhaps Suzanne is not remembering all the taxicab stories of Blacks well-dressed enough for the cabs to stop, but of course they do not. Our public intellectuals have shared their jokes arising from such situations. In his preface to the aforementioned *Race Matters*, West speaks of standing on Sixtieth Street and Park Avenue trying to catch a cab, so as to be on time to meet the photographer who will take his picture for the cover of his book. He watched nine taxis go by and a tenth taxi pick up a white woman standing near him.[9] Similarly, Henry Louis Gates Jr. writes: "It's important to remember that 'race' is *only* a sociopolitical category, nothing more. At the same time—in terms of its practical performative force—that doesn't help me when I'm trying to get a taxi on the corner of 125th and Lenox Avenue. ('Please sir, it's only a metaphor.')"[10] Race is the metaphor that people of color live every day. Race is a metaphor until its consequences affect you.

Although a writer, Suzanne maybe failed to remember Frank Marshall Davis's short poems on educated Blacks: a Mr. Giles Johnson, who despite having four college degrees and the ability to "orate in Latin 'or cuss in Greek,'" starves to death "because he wouldn't teach / and he couldn't porter." Or perhaps Suzanne does not remember Davis's "Robert Whitmore," who after achieving the American Dream "died of apoplexy / when a stranger from Georgia / mistook him/ for a former Macon waiter." [11]

To those she writes for, Suzanne, although a middle-class American writer who can lecture on "The Construction of a Play with Aristotelian Elements," is simply a whining, bothersome Black mother. Her abilities to appreciate the Antioch production of *Hamlet* or understand the classical elements of tragedy do not give her any cultural currency with Police Officer Holzer. Suzanne writes the county manager, her senators, the NAACP, and the governor. We are always ex-slaves trying to write ourselves a pass to freedom. I write you, as feverishly as Suzanne writes, to save your life. Last night when I watched the police in the play beat Teddy, I heard a white student near me whisper to another white student: "Why is this production so long?" It was long because of a long legacy of state violence against Black masculinity, a legacy of hearing "assume the position," once too often.

I write you because you are as vulnerable as Teddy was. I am both embarrassed and pained to tell you that Emmett's ghost still hovers over whatever dreams you may have. For me to say that "we are an outstanding Black American family"[12] is as hollow as Suzanne's pleas. Despite the middle-class status of your family (remember being teased that your parents' PhD and JD degrees must mean we are the Cosby family?), you have elected to wear those name-brand shirts and shoes that in our commodification of culture society have marked you as Black. You use your hair to make a statement that your lips cannot articulate. But like Teddy's mother, I worry most about what might happen to you while driving—what we call DWB (driving while Black). As innocent teenaged males, you have souped up your Hondas. You tell me that you do not have a muffler; you have an exhaust system. You have drilled strobe lights into your headlights and added hyperwhite lights that mirror different colors at different angles. You lowered your cars' suspension springs, installed a body kit, tinted your windows, added a carbon filter wing, a carbon fiber hood, cold air intake and fuel devices, and seventeen-inch racing aluminum alloys with special rims and tires with accompanying advertising decals.

You think that your father and I have resisted these changes because we have no appreciation for your cruising with the fellas, or "chillin." No, we worry that in situations like Teddy's, your education and background might lead you to take Teddy's action: "I was trying to engage him [Police Officer Holzer] in a civil conversation and I just wanted to find out what seemed to be the problem."[13] Often, Black men have thought these are situations where reason and truth will prevail. They think that if they sound articulate, they will be heard.

For your father's birthday, I gave him a copy of *The Innocents* (2003), the book based on the Innocence Project that has used DNA evidence to exonerate over a hundred men, mostly Black.[14] When I read their stories, I see that if you happen to look "thuggish," if you happen to be wearing your do-rag to keep your braids in place, you set up yourself for misidentification. Take note that in 1987 Anthony Robinson began serving ten years of a twenty-seven-year sentence because a University of Houston woman identified him as her on-campus rapist. Although DNA tests would later prove he could not have committed the crime, "the prosecution relied mainly on the victim's cross-racial identification, and Robinson was convicted of sexual assault."[15] In a postprison interview, Robinson talks about how as a Black man he must now live defensively; he must dress and behave as if he one day will face another accusation:

> Since the incident occurred, I've taken on the affectation of making sure I'm presentable when I go somewhere. It's kind of stifling for me 'cause I'm really a casual guy. But if you don't dress up in such a manner as to say, "Okay, I'm a normal person," the opportunity is there for them to say whatever they want: "He fits the description." Very rarely is somebody going to say: "He was wearing a shirt, a tie, a pair of slacks, and some hard-soled shoes."[16]

Robinson goes on to say how he documents everywhere he goes. He keeps all sorts of records, "general notations, little scraps of papers" because "my fear is if I stop, it might happen again. . . . Don't take this the wrong way, but it's kind of hard for a Black man to live in Texas and not believe in God. That's the only way you can make rational sense of the irrational things that are happening around you."[17]

There is a force out there embedded in what Houston Baker Jr. calls his "blue/black memory," a boogeyman from his Black southern childhood, a Blue Man, "stealthy, yet ferocious, fanged and vicious in pursuit of young black men."[18] All types of horrible incidents, including the murder of Emmett Till, continuously sustained the belief in the existence of such a Blue Man. Teddy/Adam, Suzanne/Adrienne, and your daddy and I all believe in the Blue Man. We believe that anything can happen, especially south of the Mason-Dixon Line. Blue Men might have helped Dick and Jane cross the street, but they have been known to leave young Black boys as roadkill. In writing about the O. J. Simpson case, Toni Morrison contends: "For middle and upper classes the police are the praetorian guard. They are the men in blue who riot for them, in place of them, who are implacable in their pursuit of the disorderly, the unhoused and the criminal, and who sometimes have to violate law to enforce it. For whites to consider police corruption as systemic rather than occasional is to place themselves in the untenable position of being shielded *by*, rather than protected from, chaos."[19]

Suzanne writes Teddy, Adrienne wrote Adam, and I write you because as Houston Baker Jr. says, "Writing [is] our black defense against and revision of ancient terrors, mistaken identities, dread losses. . . . If needed, we [can] summon an articulate revisionary grace against the assaults of men in all-American blue, who would, on some indeterminate future sunny day, arrest, insult, pin us down on the all-purpose white man's charge: 'You are hereby charged for blackness ... the nigger in you!'"[20] *Sleep Deprivation Chamber* is a frame story embedded with stories from two plays with murders, Adrienne Kennedy's own *The Ohio State Murders* and Shakespeare's *Hamlet*. Ultimately, the play is not as much about the beating or the potential for murder as it is about what legal theorist Patricia Williams calls *spirit-murder*: "disregard for others whose lives qualitatively depend on our regard ... its product is a system of formalized distortions of thought. It produces social structures centered around fear and hate; it provides a tumorous outlet for feelings elsewhere unexpressed."[21] Williams goes on to declare that spirit-murder should be a capital moral defense.

Sons, the truth is that we are afraid that your cars, your dress, your behaviors might one day place you in Teddy's crouching position, pleading, "Sir, I can't breathe ... I'm an American citizen, could you please let me up and breathe?"[22] Our concern is that your life not be a sleep deprivation chamber and that you not go through experiences that murder your spirit and conjure our blue/Black memories.

Thrive,
Your mother

———————————

December 5, 2014: eleven years later

To my twenty-eight-year-old twin sons, Adam and Andrew:

"I can't breathe. I can't breathe. I can't breathe. I can't breathe. I can't breathe."

Figure 2.1. Lee Twins. My sons, Adam and Andrew Lee, at twenty-eight years old enjoying an audience of fans after their appearance on a TV episode of *House Hunters*. Photo taken outside of a mall in Dallas, Texas, October 16, 2014.

Here you are. Although I am not a good photographer, I have managed to capture you walking from a mall. Others approach you and ask for your autograph because you have appeared on a television reality show. You are twenty-eight years old. Although you are always handsome, smart, and independent, I need to reiterate something that I wrote you years ago. This time, it is no longer Teddy crying out for justice in a play. It is now real-life Eric Garner, a forty-three-year-old Black man in Staten Island, New York, trying to live while trapped in a chokehold by a white police officer. Suspecting that Garner might have been selling untaxed cigarettes, the officers restrained him, and while Garner was gasping for breath, repeating eleven times, "I can't breathe," they did not administer CPR. With others worldwide, I watch the video, and it is déjà vu all over again.

It is now real-life Michael Brown, an eighteen-year-old Black man in Ferguson, Missouri. It is now real-life John Crawford, a twenty-two-year-old Black man in Beavercreek, Ohio, shot while examining a gun on a Wal-Mart shelf. It is now real-life Ezell Ford, a twenty-five-year-old mentally ill Black man in southern Los Angeles, shot during an "investigative stop." It is now real-life Tamir Rice, a twelve-year-old Black child on a Cleveland playground, cellphone in one hand and toy plastic pellet gun in another, shot at point-blank range within two seconds of the rookie officer's arrival on the scene. Implicit bias research tells us that Black children appear older in the eyes of the Other. How *old* can a twelve-year-old look? How old did teenager Trayvon Martin, walking by a gated community with a bag of Skittles in his pockets, look to George Zimmerman? My eyes teared up the next morning when I walked into my university's Black Cultural Center, and on the walls someone had written, Long Live Zimmerman.

I know you are much older now, and you don't want me to worry. You might even think me paranoid (like Uncle Juju who always thought the FBI and CIA were spiking his coffee or Auntie who still thinks that the story of white men landing on the moon is a hoax). It is not paranoia; it is just that as a teacher, I know when a class roster is too long, and this one is. I can barely keep track of the Black and Brown bodies going down unarmed, unheard, and unvindicated. I used to worry about the Deep South. But Ferguson, Staten Island, Los Angeles, Beavercreek, and Cleveland challenge my geographical assumptions.

What can I say to you now? Your father and I are embarrassed and dis-appointed that our generation did not get things done. By many standards we have done our job; you are well adjusted, well rounded, well educated, and well employed. Yet I would be remiss if I failed to admit that, like many others from our generation, your father and I dedicated so much attention to keeping you safe and happy at home that we neglected to take further strides in making the world a happier and safer space for you. And while I know that we are not solely capable of correcting that which has remained undone for so long, my parental responsibilities to you sometimes encourage me to wish that we all would have done more. Adam and Andrew, you always have been proud of us, but now we must by necessity disclose that no matter how many times we told you the proverbial booster "You can be and do anything," we still harbored racialized fears. So, I am back to asking you to be careful: place your hands up, keep your mouth closed, make no quick moves, shine your shoes, wipe your nose, untwist your locked hair, clean your teeth, shave your goatee, do whatever it takes to live while Black. Practice what protestors of police violence are calling a "die-in." Pretend to be dead. And if that is too cowardly a task to perform, if that is the life you cannot live, then in your protest, promise me that you will anchor your beliefs in foundations strong enough to sustain you.

I am proud that both of you are well employed in corporate America (only occasionally asking your father and me for any kind of loan), but surely you know by now that you do not have the same freedoms as the young white male professionals with whom you attend your morning meetings, collaborate on team projects, and work out at the gym. They can sell untaxed cigarettes or any number of items and not be guilty of a capital crime. They can afford to play with guns missing the orange toy safety cap. They can examine guns that sit on the shelves of retail stores or play with toy guns on playgrounds, but you must never. A toy gun, or knife, or any sharp instrument in your hands will be misread. You are always already violent, guilty, and disposable.

The chances are strong that one day you will hear officers telling you to "assume the position." Your father and I would rather you be careful so that it never comes to that situation, but if it does, we hope you will have enough spiritual strength to place America in a chokehold.

Hands up, Don't Shoot, Black Lives Matter,
Your mother[23]

Smarts

A CAUTIONARY TALE

"Of course, one of the dangers of standing at an intersection—particularly at such a suddenly busy, three-way intersection—is the likelihood of being run over by oncoming traffic."—Ann duCille, *Skin Trade*

Background

There is a tradition among some of the colleges at my university to ask those promoted to full professorship to give an inaugural lecture for their colleagues and invited guests. These lectures start with a short summary of the professor's research profile, and then one has the freedom to give a summary of future projects or say whatever one wants at this professional milestone. For my talk, after summarizing the content and context of my most recent book, I decided to cut to the heart of how the academy defines such terms as "success," "intelligence," or what I called "smarts." That is, after successfully meeting the criteria for promotion without any hiccups, I wanted the academy to know that I was always listening to another set of criteria: one that was at times critical of academe's criteria. I chose the promotion-to-full inaugural lecture as the moment in time to make a university-wide public statement on privilege, authority, entitlement, knowledge systems, or simply "smarts." By critiquing academe at the very time that I entered its most hallowed halls, I was at best performing what African American poet Thylias Moss refers to in her poetry collection, *Last Chance for the Tarzan Holler*. "Last Chance for the Tarzan Holler" is whatever you grapple with the moment before entering some final passage, the moment before any life-changing event. It is a holler that "affirms and resists the very [situation] that it heralds."[1] At worst, the moment of promotion to full professor is when one finally receives what Mari Evans calls in her poem, "Status Symbol," "the key to the white locked john." It was at this moment in my career, the passage from associate to full, that I decided to share my strategy for engagement with my white colleagues, who had all come to praise "her fullness." It was time to reveal that although I had played by all the rules, I never bought their definition of "smarts." Here I share that speech:

INAUGURAL FULL PROFESSOR ADDRESS

Earlier Scholarship

As an African American scholar in the academy, I have been negotiating traffic at a busy intersection for the last twenty-five years. For me, race, gender, class, disability, sexuality, and a range of categories of social difference have not been faddish, fast-moving sports cars on an academic highway. Rather, they have been the permanent routes, however fluid and contested, that I have chosen to pursue. As if traveling the routes of social difference were not enough, I have followed an itinerary that has been further complicated by a joint appointment in English and women's studies, as well as courtesy appointments in the departments of African American and African studies, comparative studies, and the Center for Folklore Studies. This type of inter-disciplinarity and intersectionality has demanded that I have a clear sense of methodologies and theoretical frameworks for my research. Confronting promotion and tenure committees with anything less than knowing what I am doing and how I am doing it would have left me as *roadkill* on academe's outer belt—never arriving close enough to its city of power to make any difference. So, I have been strategic about my analytical tools and the arguments that I have formulated that allow me to employ those tools.

In *Granny Midwives and Black Women Writers: Double-Dutched Readings*, I demonstrate what it means to pursue research at the nexus of race, gender, culture, and class and create an accommodating methodology. I began my research with the question: why do the novels of so many contemporary African American women writers contain portraits of Black lay midwives and women healers who are simultaneously constructed as obstetricians, chemists, rootworkers, and psychotherapists? In pursuing this question, I realized that I would have to study the historical lives of the many southern, rural African American women who during their heyday, the 1920s and 1930s, numbered more than forty-three thousand and who, although described in some government publications as "uncompetent nigra women," in their own communities, "stood as tall as God."[2] I had decided to tell the historical grannies' stories in tandem with the fictional representations of their stories. However, my first roadblock was that at the time that I was doing my book, no one had written about the lives of the Black lay midwives. There was one book on one particular granny midwife,[3] but there were no collected histories of their lives. I could not believe that these women, who had delivered thousands of Black and white babies, who birthed and healed a nation, had not commanded scholarly attention. How was I to do what I wanted to do with the literature when the history was not there? Scholars of color in the academy often must first fill vacuums before they can do their work.

Although I had not originally planned to do all the archival and ethnographic work, I had to do it. If there was "no there there," as Gertrude Stein would say, then I had to do the research that would validate the lives of the Black lay midwives as a first step to understanding how their lives resonated with the literary characterizations of a long list of conjure women: Toni Morrison's Pilate (*Song of Solomon*) and Marie-Therese (*Tar Baby*); Gloria Naylor's Sapphira Wade and Mama Day (*Mama Day*); Toni Cade Bambara's Minnie Ramson (*The Salt Eaters*); Tina McElroy Ansa's *Baby of the Family*; selected Alice Walker short stories, and many other authors and texts. I had to bring together the medical history, the cultural history, and the literary tradition in a way that my colleagues in the discipline of English would find credible and a way that I felt was culturally responsive to the material. My task was to talk about all of these *sistah conjurers* without sounding like a conjure woman myself. For although I knew that the original meanings of "conjure" were closely associated with *double-headed* and *double wisdom*,[4] thus an empowering idiom for diasporic sisterly powers, I could not count on my colleagues to read *conjure* apart from its European-inflected meanings of Black witchcraft. Scholars of color in the academy are always suspect.

I wanted a methodology that would fit my subject matter. It had to be a methodology that was grounded in multiplicities, able to accommodate my project's interdisciplinarity. It also had to be a methodology that was at ease with a culturally grounded text. I wanted to follow in the footsteps of African American scholars who were using Indigenous metaphors for writing African American experiences: Elsa Barkley Brown's "quilting" of history; Henry Louis

Gates Jr.'s "speakerley texts"; Mae Henderson's "speaking in tongues" trope; and bell hooks and Cornel West's "breaking bread" metaphor. I wanted my methodology to travel to what Karla Holloway calls a "cultural mooring place."[5] One day, while sitting at the kitchen table with a laptop, a PC, and a printer, I noticed my daughters in the driveway jumping double-dutch. As I watched the turning of multiple ropes, listened to their chanting of folk rhymes, and saw them negotiate space between the two ropes in front of a company of neighbors waiting their turn, I knew that I was witnessing the performance of my methodology. Here was an art form closely associated with the experiences of young Black girls. In *Granny Midwives*, I transform jumping double-dutch into a practice of reading dual cultural performances, the performances of the historical grannies, and the performances of the literary texts. Just as jumping double-dutch requires the jumpers to listen to the chanting and sound of the ropes, then multiply locate themselves between ropes, I ask my readers to hear the orality of the two sets of texts and multiply locate themselves between my narrative ropes.[6]

Jumping double-dutch is much harder than merely skipping rope. It requires a company, a community of jumpers. It is difficult to learn, for one must perform a set of verbally sung instructions while the two ropes are turning. Jumping in requires a number of false starts. Jumpers sway their bodies back and forth as they try to match the rhythm of the ropes. Building on double-dutch as a trope, I discuss the ropes of my analysis as an intertextual, interplay performed against a polyphonic range of Black women's voices, providing the interdisciplinary freedom my work requires.

Not having found a methodology that complemented my role as an "Indigenous ethnographer," I risked creating one. One of the benefits of having done so is watching how others who practice women-of-color feminisms have made use of the model. Imagine my surprise when someone sent me a tape of a womanist theologian who spoke at a large convention and introduced her work as "double-dutched ministry," citing the work that I had done. In addition to the methodological work, the historical recovery work has attracted an audience. Medical groups such as Lamaze International and Midwives Alliance of North America (MANA) have asked me to participate as a speaker at their national or regional conventions. Although I never planned to build bridges between medicine and literature, there was work that needed to be done, a gap that needed to be filled.

Just as rewarding as academic and professional responses has been the response from African American communities. Interdisciplinary work and methodologies that resonate with frameworks familiar to one's home community engage populations outside the academy. Perhaps it was the Varnette Honeywood picture of young people jumping double-dutch on the cover of *Granny Midwives* that caught the attention of the editors of the hip-hop magazine *Vibe*. In any event, in the special Notorious B. I. G. death keepsake issue there's a review of *Granny Midwives* as a text that does cultural work. The practice within my department is to place reviews on a bulletin board. Usually the reviews are from canonical, professionally approved journals. I had the pleasure of tacking on the wall the *Vibe* review, a review that placed *Granny Midwives* next to books with titles that usually do not grace the hallowed walls of academe: *Tough Love: Cultural Criticism and Familial Observations on the Life and Death of Tupac Shakur* and *Fuck You Too, the Extras+More Scrapbook*. Scholars of color in the academy often go where no one has gone before.

Smarts

When one does work that engages a range of categories of difference, when one theorizes difference and diversity, the academy does not always see such an endeavor as smart. What happens when one finds oneself caught between two intellectual traditions, caught between communities that define "intellectual" in different ways? How does one negotiate separate communities when what one community calls "presence of mind," the other calls "stoned out of one's mind"? Many scholars, especially scholars of color who practice Black feminist criticism, have dual allegiances. Their home communities expect them to "give back and reach back"; yet they work in structures where their success depends on how well they can distance themselves from that community. As such, Black feminist scholars become Trojan horses[7] in the academy, doing what Chandra Mohanty would call oppositional work with institutional space.

Historically, African Americans often have shaped knowledge from different interpretive frameworks. Most academic units have shared and written notions of what excellence in teaching, research, and service means. Prior to the times when scholars of color presented their calling cards at the academy's door, faculty members were pretty smug about the meanings of such words and phrases as "canon," "rigor of thought," "cutting edge," and "the educated mind." Contrastingly, a survey of African American folk stories and literature reveals a distinction between education and *edumacation*. The space between the two concepts is a contradictory space, as most complex spaces are. That is, even as most African American communities have praised literacy and education as the way to freedom and success, there has always been another discourse that says you have to watch out for white folks' education, book learning, derisively called *edumacation*. In Ebonics, the extra syllables indicate pomposity, extremity, as when Langston Hughes's character, Jesse B. Simple, calls worry, "worriation." Worry can stress you out, but worriation can kill you. *Edumacation* is academe's corruption of smartness. *Edumacation* is what folks at home think you are getting when they start asking, "Now how long have you been in school? What degree did you say are you working on *now*?" *Edumacation* calls into question many of academe's ironclad canons.

Take for example Jessica Care Moore's poetry. Why is it that at the Apollo, where one misspoken word or note can get one laughed off stage, so many of the new hip-hop poets are bringing down the house with poems about learning and scholars? How is it that Jessica Care Moore, the poet who has an unheard-of winning record of five weeks in a row at the Apollo Theater's Amateur Night Slam Nation Competition, has touched audiences with poems not only about drugs, violence, poverty, or some other stereotypical subject matter but also with poems about T. S. Eliot, the grand old man of modernism? Moore dedicates "There Are No Asylums for the Real Crazy Women" to Vivienne, T. S. Eliot's wife. The poem begins by calling Eliot "an English tea drinking dog / Who quietly and without remorse / Stole his wife's spirit." At another point in the poem, Eliot is an "Anglo nerd knight of the canon kings."[8] What happens when as a professor of literature, you find yourself caught between one intellectual tradition that says T. S. Eliot is the father of a noble tradition and the other that calls him "an English tea drinking dog," and "Anglo nerd knight of the canon kings"? How does one read the multiple discourses at the nexus of race, gender, and culture? Is the academy the only audience to whom one has to answer? How can anyone learn to read something as contingent and contentious as race?

In a piece entitled, "Unleash the Queen," Marlon Riggs irreverently critiques the academy's attempt to certify him as Race and Sexuality Resident expert: Can Miss Thing "comprehend discursive intertextual analysis, can she engage in postfeminist, neo-Marxist, postmodern deconstructionist critique? Does she understand the difference between text, subtext, and metatext? Does she know she's part of a subaltern universe? Can she, in a word, *really* read?"[9] In the essay, Riggs speaks of academe as a place where he gives his most prize-winning performances. Like Moore's poetry, his words echo the distinction between education and *edumacation*. *Edumacation* is using a critical vocabulary to dazzle one's audience. Education is understanding that critical vocabulary well enough to choose simpler, common words.

Smarts in African American Folklore and Literature

As a parent of four teenagers, I have attended a number of middle and high school graduation ceremonies in recent years. One folk story that I have heard repeatedly at commencement services at predominately Black schools is one that warns of where *edumacation* can lead to. Even as the Black speakers praise the students for their accomplishments, they caution them with such stories as the one about the boy, the scholar, and the minister. It's a flight story, as so many stories in African American folklore and literature are, and there are many variations of the story. A white minister, a young African American boy, and a white scholar board a small plane. The white scholar is Dr. So-and-So with an expertise in Such-'n'-Such. His research is rigorous, groundbreaking, risk-taking. When the plane is having engine trouble, all three passengers must parachute to safety. There are two parachutes and three passengers. The scholar immediately grabs a parachute, exclaiming that the world cannot afford to lose his expertise. With one parachute left, the minister, exercising his Christian virtues, tells the young boy that he may have the remaining parachute. They argue back and forth because the young boy keeps insisting that they both can parachute to safety. When the minister asks him why he feels that way, the little boy replies: "You know Dr. So-and-So with all those degrees, who said the world couldn't live without his brains? Well, that wasn't a parachute he grabbed. That was my backpack."

A contemporary folk story that circulated to Black literary listserv groups is another flight story. This time the plane is a large plane with all white passengers, except for an African American mother and her daughter. When the plane begins to have engine trouble, the white pilot throws off cargo to lessen the weight. Still the plane is too heavily loaded. The pilot must throw people off. Thinking to get rid of the African American mother and daughter first, the white pilot announces that he is going to throw passengers off in alphabetical order. He voices what sounds like a racially neutral policy, "When I call the alphabet of your identity, please step forward." He calls out, "A." The woman and her daughter remain seated. He calls out "B." Although obviously Black, the woman and her daughter still remain seated. Frustrated, the pilot calls, "C"—thinking certainly the mother and daughter will recognize themselves as colored. When the mother fails to move, the daughter says, "Ma, I thought we were African American, Black, and colored." Clinging to her seat more tightly, the Black mother tells the daughter, "Today, we are Negroes." Smarts is resourcefulness. It is what one uses to dodge bullets, lynching mobs, and public policy schemes that have racist effects.

SMARTS AND "OLD MASSA" STORIES

Slavery generated a canon of stories that posited smarts as one-upmanship on some beast (usually mules, foxes, rabbits, and buzzards) and one-upmanship on "old massa." As such, smarts is relational. Staying ahead of massa constitutes smartness. One such story is about the slave, John, and his master. Massa wakes up one morning and tells John that he went to "nigger heaven," but he didn't have a good time because everyone was loud, the place was dirty, and a host of other stereotypical details. John quietly listens and then tells his master that he had a dream, too. In John's dream, he goes to "white heaven." John reports that everything was neat and clean, the streets pearly and white. But, as John explains, "Dey wuzn't uh soul in de whole place." [10]

This type of traditional *outsmarting whitey story* is not unlike the contemporary stories that emphasize smarts as using common sense to settle matters that whites in authority find baffling. For 101-year-old and 103-year-old African American sisters Elizabeth and Sarah Delany in *Having Our Say*, old massa becomes Congress, a group of men easily outsmarted. Elizabeth writes of her ability to make judgments that white congressmen found difficult:

> That Clarence Thomas mess, the Supreme Court nomination. He's lying. That girl, Anita Hill, is telling the truth. And Sadie says, "How do you know?" Well, I'll tell you something, Honey, I know a rascal when I see one! Sadie and I watched the whole thing on the TV, and when I saw all those silly old white men asking those stupid questions I almost got myself on a train and went down to Washington. I could have straightened out that whole Clarence Thomas mess in ten minutes, yes sir! I should have gotten myself on a train and gone on down there but Sadie wouldn't let me. [11]

SMARTS AND INDIVIDUAL AND SYSTEMIC RACISM:

I'll tell you what takes real intelligence—dealing with people's
ignorance. Crazy questions that white people ask.

—BLACK WOMAN FROM NORTH CAROLINA
(*Streetsmart & Motherwise*)

Many folk stories and jokes argue that smarts is knowing how to deal with individual and systemic racism. The many DWB (Driving while Black) stories admonish their listeners to smarten up. According to these stories, in a racialized world African Americans need to know that when driving, they are as likely to get a ticket for DWB as for anything else. The DWB stories are numerous. Willie Gary, a well-known African American attorney, tells one such story that combines literacy and racial profiling. He tells of driving south in the late 1960s in a nice car when a white southern cop pulls him over. Remembering that he did not have his driver's license on him, he feverishly pulls out the first card in his wallet. Upon seeing that it is his NAACP membership card, Gary fears he will be lynched for sure. Not only is he driving an expensive car, but he has also just offered evidence of what he imagines the cop will consider a radical political group. The cop takes the card, looks intently at it, and says, "Boy, this is a funny looking license; you go on and don't come back." The cop could not read.[12]

SMARTS IN AFRICAN AMERICAN LITERATURE

As with African American folklore, African American literature redefines "smarts." In Ralph Ellison's *Invisible Man,* the protagonist at an all-Black school controlled by white trustees is supposed to show the trustee around campus. He takes the trustee to a place where the Black school president did not want the trustee to go. It is a place where so-called poor, ignorant Blacks reside. Although the trustee turns out to have the same sexual appetites as the poor ignorant Black farmer he is taken to visit, the Black college president is angry with the very scholarly student who mistakenly carries the trustee to the wrong side of town. The president is furious that the protagonist has revealed to the trustee this side of Black life. Angry, the president rants, "The dumbest black bastard in the cotton patch knows that the only way to please a white man is to tell him a lie! What kind of education are you getting around here?"[13] The protagonist was making progress toward his degree, but he isn't smart enough to pick up on racial relations—so he is expelled.

Smarts is resiliency. Characters such as Langston Hughes, Alberta K. Johnson, and Jesse B. Simple are savvy folks who make it in life because they have managed to keep their wits despite forces that seek to demolish them. As Simple explains,

I have been fired. Laid off, and last week given an indefinite vacation, also Jim Crowed, segregated, barred out, insulted, eliminated, called black, yellow, and red, locked in, locked out, locked up, also left holding the bag. I have been caught in the rain, caught in raids, caught short with my rent, and caught with another man's wife. (And if that's not enough): I have been underfed, underpaid, undernourished, and everything but undertaken.... I been abused, confused, misused, false-arrested, tried, sentenced, paroled, blackjacked, beat, third-degree, and near about lynched. I was born with the measles! Since then I had the smallpox, chicken pox, whooping cough, appendicitis, athlete's foot, tonsillitis, arthritis, backache, mumps, and a strain—but I am still here. Daddy-o, I'm still here.[14]

Simple refuses to let obstacles stop him from moving forward in life. He walks urban streets dispensing wisdom, arguing for an alternative type of knowledge and accountability, much like the characters in Toni Cade Bambara's "The Lesson" do. Told through the voice of a young Black girl in an urban environment, the story is about a teacher who takes her class to FAO Schwartz, the very expensive toy store. She wants to teach her poor, urban students about economics and class privilege. Her lesson is patronizing and cruel, for she assumes that her students, Flyboy, Junebug, Q. T., Sugar, Fat Butt, and the rest have been too ignorant to conceptualize their position in society. The teacher, Miss Moore, gives each child $5 to spend and emphasizes that this is real money. The narrator complains that "Miss Moore asking us do we know what real money is, like we a bunch of retards. I mean real money, she say, like it's only poker chips or monopoly papers we lay on the grocer."[15] After a wild cab ride, where the kids start making all kinds of unmentionable sounds with their armpits, they finally arrive at the store. When they see the high prices, one student asks, "Can we steal?"[16] Dispirited by their own lack of resources, one student inquires, "Watcha bring us here for, Miss Moore?"[17] When Miss Moore asks the students what they learned, their response is: "White folks crazy."[18] Rather than have their difference judged as a deficit, the students make statements that validate their meager but sensible negotiation of goods and services.

Scholars, whether Black or white, often become targets of critique and ridicule in African American literature. Gloria Naylor's Reema's boy in *Mama Day* goes to college and returns home with erroneous and extravagant theories to explain everyday life. When he tells his hometown that he is doing *field*work, they mockingly point out that he "ain't never picked a boll of cotton or head of lettuce in his life."[19] They question his use of the term *field* and mockingly perform their roles as native informants by spitting tobacco in his tape recorder and other such antics. It is not the experience of college that the novel devalues. Rather, it is the arrogance that assumes that one's home communities that have survived slavery and its aftermath are ignorant. Nikki Giovanni's "Alabama Poem," demonstrates the clash. A college coed walks down a dusty road and meets an elderly Black man and an elderly Black woman. The old man shouts out to her, "Girl! My hands seen / more than all / them books they got / at Tuskegee," and the old woman tells her "My feet / seen more than yo eyes / ever gonna read." The warning here is to make use of hands and feet that know cultural terrain as a site of struggle.

A number of African American novels speak about the damage that some white scholars routinely do when they analyze the world from what they see as a neutral standpoint. Adam Nehemiah, the white historian in Sherley Anne Williams's *Dessa Rose,* tries to write Dessa's story of rebellion from the perspective of someone who can only imagine the slave woman as "darky" and "wench." The history he writes competes with the history written on Dessa's body—a body where a whip has lashed a tale "writ among her privates." At the story's end, Adam, distraught over the fact that no one believes him when he identifies Dessa as an escaped slave, is an indictment of all would-be scholars who take it upon themselves to commodify and colonize the experience of others.

Even more disconcerting is the white educator called "schoolteacher" in Toni Morrison's *Beloved.* As a scholar, schoolteacher has kept a ledger of Sethe's human and animal characteristics. Instead of a redneck overseer, *Beloved* uses schoolteacher, a man of learning, to show how one is required to be complicit in one's own destruction, as Sethe was required to make the ink for schoolteacher's writings. Sethe also understands that scholars such as schoolteacher can "dirty you so bad you couldn't like yourself anymore. Dirty you so bad you forgot who you were and couldn't think it up."[20] Schoolteacher's and Adam Nehemiah's methodologies do not work in emancipatory ways for Sethe's and Dessa's lives. Each woman has to map out a different terrain for her life. And therein lies a cautionary tale. In *Yo' Mama's DisFunktional!: Fighting the Culture Wars in Urban America*, Robin D. G. Kelley argues that scholars and policymakers play the dirty dozens with Black people's lives. By blaming Black women and Black family structures instead of indicting institutional racism, Kelley argues that scholars have done more to talk about Black people's mamas than anyone else.[21]

In sum, I created a methodology that resonates with the lives of many African Americans because I wanted to close the distance between how race, gender, and culture are discussed in the academy and how African American lives are lived outside the academy. To do so I had to recognize that there are experts in both camps. Scholars of color who cut off their home communities lose a valuable resource. Alice Walker's poem, "For My Sister Molly Who in the Fifties," describes how her older sister was transformed by college, learning new words and new concepts, but whose transformation failed to do anything for her family and home community other than make them feel like country bumpkins. The poem does not fault Molly because her education took her to many different places; it faults her because she did not know how to travel to those places and travel home again. The poem is a good companion piece to Walker's story, "Everyday Use," which makes a case for going one step further than merely using cultural artifacts, such as quilts, to adorn one's college room. In the story one daughter, Dee, wants her grandmother's quilts because they are good grassroots symbols of a poverty-stricken backwoods past from which she has distanced herself; however, that past is in vogue. The other daughter, Maggie, who did not go to college, wants the quilt because as Dee tells us, Maggie is "backward enough to make them everyday use."[22]

Today, in many Black churches, even as the congregations praise the accomplishments of their graduate students, they take great joy in pointing out that the PhD stands for "pray heaven delivers." It's quite common for graduates to give a testimony where they claim that although some have graduated *cum laude, magna cum laude, summa cum laude,* they are thankful simply to have graduated "praise the lawdy." Laughter usually follows these declarations, not to belittle the achievement but to affirm that the graduates have not let their education become *edumacation* and to signify that they are planning to do something transformative with their "smarts"—like put it to everyday use.

On Learning That I Was Teaching "N----r Literature"

OR WHY IT'S HARD TO DO DIVERSITY IN ACADEME

It's June 1999, six months before the new millennium. I'm on a plane headed for the National Women's Studies Conference in Albuquerque, New Mexico, with a stopover in Dallas. Seated beside me is a seventeen-year-old white girl who is completing her first round-trip plane ride. She has just visited her father's house in Chillicothe, Ohio, and is returning home to a small town outside Dallas. Still apprehensive about flying, she chatters nonstop. Imagining my own daughter who was also seventeen years old at the time, I listen patiently as she explains how free she feels in Chillicothe. She describes everything about the boyfriend back home: their plans to marry upon graduation, the community college both plan to attend, and their plans to then transfer to a four-year institution. I hear all about what the other girls in the class think about her, the teacher who graded her unfairly, and the off-the-shoulder dress she is planning to wear to senior prom.

She is most animated when she talks about her grandparents with whom she lives. I smile as she shares the many times that she fooled them about curfew, making me wonder what lies my own daughter has told me. The picture she paints of her grandfather is one of a disciplinarian, straight out of Grant Wood's *American Gothic* painting, pitchfork and all. It saps his energy to deal with the five grandchildren in their three-bedroom house. Often, he has to give the grandchildren what my seatmate describes as "wumpings." We arrive in Dallas, and I marvel that she has taken to me instinctively, as if she knew I was the mother of four teenagers and would understand every word she was saying. I thought that I had been having what some would call a color-blind conversation. Until our final words: "Sally Ann, I hope that you and your grandfather have a good year," I said, trying to mimic the positive outlook that this long-haired blonde girl exuded. "Oh, you needn't worry about that," she responded. I'm his favorite grandchild. He loves me the most because I'm the *only pure white one.*"

Stunned, I didn't know what to say: Do I give a crash course on race as a social construction, an empty category? Do I tell her, as feminist scholar Ruth Frankenburg argues in a groundbreaking work, that "whiteness refers to a set of locations that are historically, socially, politically, and culturally produced and moreover are intrinsically linked to unfolding relations of domination. Naming 'whiteness' displaces it from the unmarked, unnamed status that is itself an effect of its dominance?"[1] Or do I share with her the work of legal scholar Ian López who reminds us that "whites do not exist as a natural group, but only as a social and legal creation"?[2] Or do I go both the naughty but hopeful route and tell her that Wray and Newitz, in their book *White Trash*, detail the class differences within whiteness and how, if historically and socially understood, these class differences could lessen racist attitudes: "differences within whiteness—differences marked out by categories like white trash—may serve to undo whiteness as racial supremacy, helping to produce multiple, indeterminate, and anti-racist forms of white identity?" The authors of *White Trash* push their claims further by asserting that "because white trash, is for whites, the most visible and clearly marked form of whiteness, it can perhaps help to make all whites self-conscious of themselves as a racial and classed group among other such groups, bringing us one step closer to a world without racial division, or, at the very least, a world where racial difference does not mean racial, symbolic, and economic domination."[3] Do I let her know that whiteness studies has already gone through several waves and her belief in the biology of whiteness is archaic?

Although the scholar in me wanted to give my seatmate a crash course in Critical White Studies 101, the mother in me wanted to affirm that I had listened to and respected her telling of her life story. We had had a good conversation, and I decided not to spoil her purity trope of her existence as a Nordic in Dallas. After all, to her "pure whiteness" was not a trope; it was blood, her very being. I move in intellectual circles where no one proclaims pure white blood or pure anything. Sally Ann's innocence and forthrightness captivated me. Although she certainly had benefited from white supremacist discourse, she was just a regular little white girl navigating her world as well as she knew how. So, instead of telling her that one of America's problems is that whiteness is still an asset, like property—and that her use of it as if it were a MasterCard, offering privileges and protection—will one day hurt my daughters, I blurt out the only question remaining in my mind:

"*If you are the only pure white one, what are the other grandchildren?*" As it turned out, her mother had children by a Mexican and an African American. The grandparents were keeping all of the children because of the mother's waywardness, her proclivity to dilute white womanhood. Although people in the hometown knew her family history and would not see Sally Ann as "pure," in Chillicothe, Ohio, Sally Ann was pure white and free. In the new millennium it has come to this: a white girl must cross the Ohio River on a jet to reach freedom and pass for "pure white."

Hold that story.

Meeting Sally Ann made me think of myself at her age. At seventeen, I entered the twelfth grade. I grew up in southern Maryland where everything is named after aristocratic British families—Lord Baltimore, Lord Calvert, Princess Anne, Prince Frederick. I would never know how silly all of these names sounded until I went away to college, and my roommate introduced herself as Betty from Harlem. She said "Harlem" with the same larger-than-life, Black Mecca overtones of a Langston Hughes protégé.

"Where are you from?"

I mumbled, "Prince Frederick."

"Prince what?" laughed Betty. Our relationship never recovered.

School integration came hard to Prince Frederick, Calvert County, Maryland. A white and Black school that had sat virtually across the street from each other now had to integrate. It was *the law*. At the time Maryland had an elaborate track system, so the way the school district obeyed the law was selecting only the "most qualified minorities" to gradually integrate into the white schools. It would take four years before all the Blacks from the Black high school would be permitted inside the white school, a school that looked like a mall. So, I sat in mostly all-white classes happy to finally get to such courses as PE (Physical Education) and "Issues in Contemporary Society"— classes that permitted real integration. We knew that race relations were a little more liberal forty miles north in Washington, DC, or as we called the city, "DC." I remember the night H. Rap Brown came through DC, and the city burned. The next morning, I am sitting in stoic Miss Gettier's class, a woman who never acknowledges the Black students in the class. Before class starts, some of the Black guys, Bootie and MC, are bragging about the shoes they looted from DC stores. Concerned about the rioting, Miss Gettier tries to involve the class in a discussion, a teachable moment. She wants the poor Black students in our class to understand that tearing down nearby poor neighborhoods is not an appropriate response. So, she calls on Bootie for the first time ever and asks him a question so stupid that even Bootie should know the answer:

"William, where is poverty?" Bootie looks around, fidgets; I start to feel embarrassed that he cannot answer a simple question:

"By golly, Bootie," I think, "Name any city—start with where we are: DC, or at least say Baltimore."

Bootie stammers, "Ah, ah, ah," and finally looks up and names a place I know he could not find on a map, a place so white, it clashes with his Black lips: "Idaho."

I laugh so much that Miss Gettier asks me to leave the room. When a teacher asks a condescending question, she deserves an unexpected answer. Yes, let's talk about class economics in Idaho. Yes, let's racialize Idaho. Just maybe the Black problem in America is the White problem in America.

Fast forward to a few days before high school graduation. (Yes, Bootie passes the course and makes it to graduation.) Several of my teachers and the school principal call me in to explain why they cannot let a Black girl be class valedictorian. It had never happened, and it would not happen on their watch. They tell me that my A grades should really have been A minuses; after all, no one is perfect. Furthermore, they explain, if they gave me straight As, they would have to do so for everyone else who did similar work. This is the same kind of argument that Jesse Owens's hometown of Oakville, Alabama, gave year after year as to why they could not erect a memorial in his honor. The city officials explained, "If we erect a statue for one man who has won four gold medals in the Olympic Games, we will have to do it for everyone from Oakville who wins four gold medals." Indeed.

A few years ago, I received an email from a white woman in my high school class. She had moved to Columbus and wanted to have lunch and discuss all the great beach parties that went on during high school. Calvert County is a peninsula with one highway leading north to Washington, DC, and all the other highways leading to rivers and the Chesapeake Bay. Many of the sites have watery names: Cypress Swamp, Bayside, Back Creek, Flag Ponds, Calvert

Cliffs. There are beaches, beaches, everywhere, but when my high school acquaintance recalled all the beach parties, I had to remind her that those were white-only beaches. All the Blacks in the town had to go to Seagull Beach, a place that when you rose out of the water, you had to pull the stinging jelly-fish off your legs. As teenage girls, we found this embarrassing. I never had lunch with that high school acquaintance. There was nothing to talk about. We had gone our separate ways. She had followed her husband to Ohio and had time on her hands to touch base with any former classmate she could find in Ohio, and I had become a professor of African American literature.

An eye-opening moment for me was that after teaching African American literature for over twenty years, I learned that what some whites thought I was doing was teaching "n----r literature." I stumbled upon this revelation while reading the autobiographical statement of a white male advisee who would later write a first-rate dissertation on race and sexuality. To this day, I am moved by the biographical essay that he wrote as part of his graduate studies admissions packet:

> I have never been a voracious reader. I take my time. I read certain pages twice. I read the same word in the same sentence over and over again trying to penetrate it. So in the summer of 2000 when I had just finished my first year of high school, I carried the same book with me everywhere, re-reading my favorite parts and mulling them over in my head.
>
> I had a job selling tickets in a small booth at an amusement park with go-karts, batting cages, and miniature golf. Business was slow on weekdays so I could bring my book and read about ten pages or so between customers. Few people talked to me then and even fewer asked about what I was reading, so when I noticed my boss eyeing the book as he approached my booth one afternoon, I worried I would get in trouble for reading and tried to hide it under a stack of papers.
>
> "That's all right. You can read," he said when he got to the booth. I felt relieved and smirked a bit while uncovering the small paperback.
>
> "What are you reading?" he asked, reaching his hand out to have a look at it.
>
> "*The Color Purple*," I said.
>
> He examined the book's front cover—a copy of the movie poster featuring Celie's violet silhouette and a big orange sun. He flipped it over to check out the back cover, and after a few seconds, as if he had suddenly remembered something, he wound his face in disgust, like what he tasted was sour.

"Why are you reading a book about a n----r?"

I was disoriented, and quickly said, "You don't have to be Black to enjoy a book about Black people." I can't remember where the conversation went from there. What I do remember is being dumbfounded, appalled, and scared. And to this day I am unsatisfied with my response to his question.

I recently went back to *The Color Purple* and noticed, for the first time, the second sentence Celie writes in the book. I suppose her self-erasure was something I had been unable to see previously, and it brought me back to my boss's question—and the question he was really asking me, through some other force: who is worthy of critical attention? My boss knew that I was white, and he insinuated that literature was white. Color, for him, tainted that solution. My idea of literature, then, was different, and I resent him for making me conscious of the fact that most of the literature I liked was written by or focused on African Americans and that, therefore, in his eyes, my interests were abnormal for a fifteen-year-old white boy.

At that moment, I understood that my boss wanted Celie and *The Color Purple* to disappear from his vision entirely. What I didn't recognize until recently is the ultimatum he posed to me—that is, either stop reading those books or you too will disappear. You will lose this job. His was an insidious attempt to have me suppress my tastes, instincts, and thoughts in order to appropriate his own psychosis onto myself. I resent him for that, too.

Part of what scared me about his question was that it was spoken so loudly. He tried to impose shame on me, and I suppose he assumed that anyone within hearing distance would share his bewilderment over what I chose to read. In this process, he got me out of that booth. He made my private experience with *The Color Purple* cause for public concern. His question had me take literature outside of that closed space, outside of my own fishbowl, and beyond my own body. He sparked a public discourse out of something that would have otherwise remained my inner monologue. Talking about literature with others has since been important to me— necessary even—in both the classroom and the street

This is why I want to earn my PhD, concentrating on cultural studies and literary theory, and eventually teach at the university level. . . . Today, I know that I would not answer a question like the one posed to me five years ago. And I would probably quit my job. But, then, I stayed there and continued to read books every summer between customers until I graduated from high school. I don't remember how to work the cash register or how to start a go-kart. I remember the books. I remember reading *The Stranger* in one day—a day so hot I thought I would pass out before I got to the last page. I read James Baldwin, Toni Morrison, and William Faulkner. Sometimes bell hooks or Cornel West. I loved those summers because of those books, but I would also worry, worry, worry that someone would ask, "What are you reading?" because of what the question had led to before. When I entered college, I began thinking critically about literature, discussing books openly, and indulging my instinct to find Celie in classic works, thereby resisting my boss's attempt to change me.[4]

This student went on to become one of the strongest students in our program as evidenced by his grades and the discursive commentary professors wrote for each of his classes.

Although the discursive comments that the department had conducted for generations of graduate students helped to give a fuller, more nuanced summary of most students' coursework, when it came to students of color, I accidentally stumbled upon evidence that the commentary worked against the spirit of diversity. As the first African American and woman chair, I wanted to nominate one of our former African American graduates to receive a prestigious Alumni Arts and Sciences Award. Although the pool was small, a high percentage of these alumni have had stellar careers. Out of respect for their privacy, I will not detail how stellar. But in browsing several files, here is what I discovered: professors, most of whom had left before I returned to the department as a faculty member, displayed implicit biases when summarizing the work of these graduate students, writing such statements as "this Negro boy has several problems stemming from his Southern HBCU background and other issues that I shouldn't have to spell out"; "'Female Student X,' having finished our Master's program, should not be admitted to our doctoral program because she is uneducable"; "'Male Student X' cannot write and tries to bring his religious convictions to every conversation"; "[Male Student X's] ear is not finely attuned to American idioms"; "[His work] was so juvenile in manner that it would have been rejected by many high school teachers; I doubt if he recognizes many intellectual issues when he sees them; he got as much out of this course as he is capable of getting"; "he is a profoundly neurotic young man."[5] I never knew that professors of English thought themselves so well versed in diagnosing mental issues until I read these graduate evaluations.

Another revelation was finding an unused funding source for our graduate students. One day, while sitting in my office, I came across a letter from a woman who had left scholarship money to the department as part of her last will and testament. The gift was very generous but came with many troubling restrictions that probably explained why the money had just been sitting in an account unused. The testator specified that she did not want any of the money to go to any users or sellers of narcotics or anyone who had been convicted of a crime. However, the restrictions did not stop there. The will stresses several times that the funds should not be given to "Negroes" or Mexicans (because "their needs are adequately provided for"), or to non-Christians (Jews). The will specifies the ideal recipients as persons of "Scandinavian extraction, at least in part." Firstly, I had not planned to distribute the scholarship money to users or sellers of narcotics. As far as not committing any crimes, I was not prepared to vouch that the graduate students had no traffic or parking tickets. As far as the exclusion of racial, ethnic, and religious groups, although the note trembled in my hand, I was not shocked that our donor did not want funds designated for Nordic literature to fall in the hands of non-Aryan, non-Christian students. After all, who does not know about restrictive housing covenants, redlining, and the long history of Jim Crow, racism, and anti-Semitism against marginalized bodies? What caught my eyes was the person the donor expected to *protect* her wishes. "I trust the Chair," she says several times in a letter. She trusted that the chair would understand what such words as "Nordic" and "Celtic" meant and would keep Brown and Black hands off the money. "I trust the Chair," our department's benefactor wrote. I do not know if she ever imagined a woman chair, but she certainly did not imagine an African American chair. She probably imagined a white male chair in a blue three-piece pinstriped suit whose mission was to preserve the sanctity of a male Eurocentric canon, faculty, and student body. "I trust the Chair"—I reread the note and kept repeating, "You can't trust the chair. Don't trust the chair. Know that one day a chair will come who will immediately work with the Office of Development to right wrongs. Know that one day a chair will come with hair twisted in braids, combing through discriminatory documents, untangling illegal knots. The benefactor probably did not imagine a day when the chair of English would have hair strands that cried, "Free at last, free at last." No, our department's benefactor never imagined a chair who looked like me.

Why did I start off by sharing stories about a young white woman finding freedom in Chillicothe, Ohio; my high school graduation story; a white male's biographical essay for doctoral study; racist discursive evaluations; and a racist bequest? Perhaps, because I love narratives and believe Native American author Leslie Marmon Silko when she says at the beginning of her novel

Ceremony that stories "aren't just entertainment / Don't be fooled. / They are all we have, you see, / all we have to fight off / Illness and death. / You don't have anything / If you don't have the stories."[6] Similarly, poet Joy Harjo infers that storytelling is "how we became human,"[7] and novelist Randall Kenan notes that "we human beings actually only have a few stories that we tell over and over again." Kenan places these stories in archetypal categories and contends that "we mix these stories up, and we turn them around and inside out."[8]

Or perhaps I shared the introductory stories because I want to make the point that talking about diversity and making diversity work are very difficult because for every story I tell that has shaped my experiences, each reader also has a story. When faculty and students sit around a seminar table, those diversity stories count in ways we do not imagine. In "Semiotics and Experience," Teresa de Lauretis reminds us that "the real difficulty, but also the most exciting, original project of feminist theory remains precisely this— how to theorize that experience, which is at once social and personal, and how to construct the female subject from that political and intellectual rage."[9] Or, as Joan Scott observes, we must learn how to historicize experience and that "it is not individuals who have experience, but subjects who are constituted through experience."[10] There are two things that we all bring to the table: our stories and our talents. The first challenge in appreciating a diverse nation is to be able to interpret and interrogate our stories.

The second challenge is not to leave any talent on the table. It is for the second reason that institutions of higher learning and corporations seek to embrace diversity more fully. And yet of all the committees that I have served on during my forty-some years in academe, there are two committees that seem to always do the same work over and over again: general education committees and diversity committees. At best, this is because this work should and must be done anew for each generation. At worst, general education committees are at a loss to pinpoint core values, and diversity committees seem faddish—something one can "wait out." As one of my former colleagues, a creative nonfiction writer and scholar in disability studies, one day remarked to me, "With diversity there is always the hope that some have that maybe it will just go away." That is, attention to diversity as an agenda item becomes just that—an item to cross off one's to-do list, the workshop one needs to attend to appease the latest student unrest group, to please the half-hearted administrative mandate, or to avoid the shame of not being seen as at least an ally. Nevertheless, I signed on to do diversity work. Chairing Ohio State

University's Diversity Council brought my career full circle. During the very first year of my professional career, I was a part of a group of faculty members at a private liberal arts institution who planned and implemented the first national general education requirement mandating that all students take a course in women's studies or Black studies prior to graduation. Yet many of the arguments I heard back then I still heard decades later but dressed in more sophisticated clothing: designer clothing, ready-to-wear clothing, dress-for-success clothing. I have been doing diversity long enough to remember when a target of opportunity meant something other than launching a Tomahawk cruise missile at leadership targets to decapitate a regime, long enough to know that cries of "reverse discrimination" are nothing more than preemptive strikes on affirmation action.

When I was chairing the University Diversity Council, we had a seven-page template of questions that we asked of all units. Some of these questions were about the unit's demographics, exit interviews, the unit's leadership composition, and so forth. We asked what administrative structures the units established to lead diversity initiatives for faculty, staff, and students and who the unit held responsible for outcomes. We requested information about recruitment and retention of women and minorities and asked what actions had been taken to make the environment for LGBTQ faculty, staff, and students safe for self-identification. In order to assess the progress of the unit, we asked the unit to follow up on our recommendations to them from the previous year. We wanted to know what procedures and programs produced results and which ones did not. All units filled out a chart that called for action steps, assessment measures, responsible persons, timelines, and dates completed. We worked hard to keep work and family issues and domestic partner benefits on the university's agenda. Our goal was that each unit be held accountable for meeting the goals of the university's Diversity Action Plan, as we sought to create a diverse university community, a community where all persons are valued and respected.

In general, our council got better at asking questions, and the responding units got better at giving answers. For example, during the first year we asked: "Is your unit's climate comfortable for LGBTQ students?" All units said their climate was "great" until we on the council wised up and asked each unit how it measured the climate and the success of its efforts. Another example: we used to ask units to comment on their efforts to diversify the professoriate. Because everyone faulted the lack of an available diverse pool, we on the council changed our question: "What steps are you taking to overcome the constraints of the pool?" Did we see progress? Let me say this: the units responded as students often do—with an uneven level of knowledge and commitment. Some units were comparable to honor students, seriously and substantively answering each question; some units mimicked students who try to improve their performance with each paper and exam. These were the units that at first did not seem to have the critical vocabulary to express their opinions, speaking of "sexual preference" and their "tolerance for diversity" or their willingness to hire "*qualified* women and minorities." These were the teachable units. Other units turned in incomplete work. The most uncooperative units were like students who simply want to quickly finish the class with a passing grade, or in the case with units, an acknowledgment that they completed the diversity survey as assigned.

And then there were units that came up with so many workable ideas that we had to make a separate document one year called "Noteworthy Initiatives." These initiatives included: curricular specializations formulated in programs organized around diversity themes; partnerships with external agencies that have diversity at the forefront of their agendas; college diversity funds; administrative fellows for women and underrepresented groups to become a part of a leadership development pool; college-wide diversity enhancement awards; college councils on diversity; a research apprenticeship program for underrepresented high school students; the development of a diversity enrichment grants program; the development of a system to track minority vendors when using a university procurement card; a week-long summer institute for college women in Ohio who are interested in public service; and many other initiatives.

Academe continues to be a community that seeks to be inclusive. My university's Diversity Council followed closely the University of Michigan's affirmative action law cases. Although the battles were costly for Michigan, as diversity often is, it certainly did not come with a price tag of $87 billion— the cost that we were paying at the time for America's historical lack of trying to understand other people of the world: in this instance, the Iraqi people. When Michigan went to battle in the *Grutter v. Bollinger* case, I yearned to be with them the way that Margaret Walker expresses in the epigraph to a short poem she wrote during the height of the civil rights movement. The epigraph expresses an actual statement that she heard an eight-year-old girl say to another young girl on the day that they were supposed to march in a protest rally. The poem, entitled "Street Demonstration," begins with an epigraph that reads, "Hurry up, Lucille or we won't get arrested with our group" and ends with "Hurry up, Lucille, Hurry up/We're going to Miss Our Chance to go to Jail."[11] There is a part of me that feels that we at my home institution missed our chance to be forever identified with a watershed decision.

"Racial difference remains America's preeminent national narrative."[12] "Talkin' the Talk and Walkin' the Walk" is a metaphor taken from sermons I have heard all my life from the pulpits of Black churches. It is a phrase that is usually spoken in the context of saints who testify, moan, roll over with the Holy Ghost while at church, but who run women, smoke weed, and party hardy all week. It is a phrase that hints at the slippage between what we believe and what we do, between what we say we value and where we place our resources and energies. As nationally-known educator and founder of Ohio State University's forty-year Graduate and Professional Day program for underrepresented groups, Dr. Frank W. Hale Jr. was fond of saying, "Commitment without cash is counterfeit."[13] It's rare to meet an academic who will say, "I don't believe in diversity." Everyone ("and his mama") believes. The problem is translating belief into practices that affect curricula, hiring, purchasing, and the full gamut of what we do. Diversity will not work unless we are willing to rethink, recreate, reappraise, and reposition our theoretical frameworks. Why not turn a discussion on reverse discrimination into one on white privilege? When someone worries that affirmative action hires may feel like tokens, turn the tables and remind them that the greatest beneficiaries of affirmative action—white males—do not feel like tokens. And if we are going to be suspicious of anyone's credentials, then it ought to be the groups that enjoy the most social, material, and political benefits. [14] Let us turn discussions about crack into discussions about powdered cocaine, let us turn discussions about Black-on-Black crime into discussions about white-on-white crime. Let us reexamine what counts as knowledge within a discipline. One of the reasons why we cannot get anywhere with diversity is we think we can come up with solutions without doing any transformative thinking. Perhaps we can learn to heed the words of James Baldwin: "Not everything that is faced can be changed, but nothing can be changed that is not faced."[15] Moreover, I gain perspective from Maya Angelou who thoughtfully suggested, "We delight in the beauty of the butterfly, but rarely admit the changes it has gone through to achieve that beauty."[16]

I continue to do research in African American women's studies with its emphases on interdisciplinary and intersectional approaches. However, as Ann duCille points out, "One of the dangers of standing at an

intersection—particularly at such a suddenly busy, three-way intersection—
is the likelihood of being run over by oncoming traffic." [17] No one wants to
be "roadkill" on academe's outer belt, so those of us who live our scholarly
lives in multiple intersections negotiate and redirect traffic as best we can.

I am well aware that discussions of diversity should bridge a number of
categories of difference, with race and gender as only two such points. I live
my life, not teasing out race and gender in neat categories, a process Toni
Cade Bambara refers to as "wasteful and dangerous splits."[18] The emphasis
within Black feminist criticism is on both/and, as in Toni Morrison speaking
of Black women as both harbor and ship.[19]

I write and talk about African American women all the time. But I want to
end with the story of a white woman who has become sort of my secret muse
ever since I found out that she existed. I had always assumed that I was the
first woman chair of the Department of English, and I know my colleagues
think that I am. But I learned something during the end of my second year of
chairing. One of my colleagues, Chris Zacher, who at the time was director of
the Humanities Institute, was poring over some archival material and found
references to a "Miss Cynthia Weld." As it turns out, Miss Weld chaired the
joint Department of History and English Language and Literature during 1883
and 1884 and was paid $120 a year. When Zacher first told me that English and
history had been one department with a woman chair, I could barely believe it.
After castigating him for poking around, for doing scholarship that dismantled
my claim to fame, I mounted up the only defense I had left: "Well, I bet you she
wasn't Black." She wasn't. The minutes from an 1885 presidential report to the
board of trustees meeting thank Miss Cynthia Weld for her service: "I wish, ...
to record my sense of the merits of Miss Weld who, at the late commencement,
left the chair of history and English. Although she came to the position under
circumstances of peculiar embarrassment, she steadily gained upon the respect
and confidence of those best qualified to judge, and at the time of her retirement was regarded by them as a capable, accomplished and successful teacher."
I have no idea what the embarrassing situation was, but I do know that Cynthia
Weld held the position as an assistant professor, and at the end of her term a
full professor from the University of Michigan, George W. Knight, took over.
In Weld's own annual report written on November 1, 1884, she too refers to "the
embarrassment inseparable from my position," in a paragraph that infers that
little was expected of her due to her rank and gender. Nevertheless, she argues
that the Department of English and History grew stronger under her leadership.

What is the point of this story? The point is that as chair of an English department that at the time had over one hundred tenured and tenure-track faculty, I planned to further my empire by reannexing the history department. No, I never want to be a colonizer. The point is that back in the 1800s, a Miss Cynthia Weld pioneered two departments that remain the largest two in the College of Humanities. I am particularly struck by the metaphor that she uses in her 1884 report to describe what constitutes a good education. She describes successful education as one with many "radiations" that extend and reach farther and farther, penetrating disciplines and cultures deeper and deeper. This is as good of a definition as any to describe what diversity does. It radiates.

In the histories of many universities there are examples of people, the Cynthia Welds, whose presences demonstrate a compelling state interest in fostering diversity. As we look to the future, higher education must remain a place where difference thrives, not because politicians, Supreme Court justices, or multiculturalists talk the talk but because we as administrators, faculty, and students are willing to walk the walk.

"Pearl Was Shittin' Worms and I Was Supposed to Play Rang-around-the-Rosie?"

AN AFRICAN AMERICAN WOMAN'S RESPONSE TO THE POLITICS OF LABOR

It is Friday, December 9, 2007, at Ohio State University. Classes for the quarter are over, so no one expects to see faculty in the halls. Yet all the tenured and tenure-track faculty members in the Department of English—all seventy of us on the Columbus campus—sit in a room, some on top of tables, some in the windowsills, waiting for a meeting to start that has the potential to change how we define, reward, and do service. Although as a department we were used to having (and indeed expected) all the senior faculty show up for promotion and tenure meetings and junior and senior faculty to show up for hiring meetings, no one would have suspected that the topic "academic service" would be enough of a magnet to attract everyone. After all, service always pales in comparison to research and teaching. Service never gets anyone tenure. It is the Clydesdale in a race run and won by thoroughbreds.

We were assembled to vote on a "workload plan." When asked by the university to institute differential teaching loads based on research productivity (allowing the mostly white male group of full professors in each college to be in a greater position to do more of what they already were doing quite well), I solicited the assistance of an associate professor and a full professor who were young enough to think creatively but experienced enough to know how to craft an argument tailored for our colleagues.[1] They went to work, creating a document that performed several functions: (1) the document made visible the fact that differential loads already existed in our unit. Many among us had course reductions for journal editing, course directorships, and internal administrative positions, such as director of undergraduate studies, graduate studies, digital media studies, and so forth. Others had contracts that gave them a course release or two, and several had private deals with the chair and/or the dean; (2) the document presented a plan whereby, without losing student enrollments (indeed increasing enrollments), everyone in the department could go on a 2-2-0 workload, which under our quarter system means six months in the classroom and six months out of the classroom; (3) the document targeted service, academic labor—not research—as the great equalizer; and (4) the document asked that we identify all activities that we value, and anyone whose civic engagement met the threshold outlined in the plan could opt for the six months in the classroom, six months out of the classroom model. Against the backdrop of a very bureaucratic institution, we had created our own in-house sabbatical.

As we sat in the room that December day, we were at a crossroads, deciding whether the historical way of doing service was in fact a model we wished to continue to institutionalize or whether we wanted to try doing service in a way that carried weight and honor. It was time for the vote. As chair of the Department of English, I had to draw upon my background as a former chair of the Department of Women's Studies to ask those most invested in our current hierarchical distribution of course releases to be willing to give those up so that we could vote for a system where everyone had an equal chance at a more desirable work/life policy. Senior white male full professors who were prolific scholars faced a tough situation. They enjoyed many opportunities that afforded them course releases, while others who taught more classes and performed as much or more service did so without the accompanying perks. The plan called for the redistribution of teaching and service expectations across the department. But to get there, the most rewarded ranks of our community had to give up some of their privileges. Of course, in the bathrooms and around the water fountains, those of us who are feminist scholars had already predicted that the heart of the issue would be about patriarchy and white privilege, however masked. But if ever there was a time when the greater good prevailed, then this meeting was the moment. Although there was some oration about meritocracy, some grandstanding about having earned an elite or a distinguished status, in the end every person present voted for the plan. It was the first time in my career that I saw colleagues teary-eyed with joy over a conversation about academic labor. At the time of this writing, the department's environment is one where people are eager to do academic labor, for the rewards are vital and visible. In a College of Humanities where everyone was on a five-course load, we had claimed our future. We voted ourselves a life.

I would like to think that this moment in time owes much to my two colleagues who bravely and dutifully drafted the plan and a little to the fact that I am the first woman and the first African American chair of a department whose roots go back to the 1880s. Moreover, I am doing this chairing at a time when my dean, who had to approve the workload plan, is an African American male with specialties that I share in African American literature and folklore. Here I am claiming a particular attitude about service that is heavily influenced by the mores of Black communities, African American folklore traditions, and African American women's literature. Academic service has been the stumbling block for many African American tenure candidates because academe has been slow in recognizing (and the candidates have been slow in relinquishing) a social contract that emphasizes the rhetoric of "reach back," "come back," and pay back." Many African American faculty grow up hearing proverbs about service, such as Shirley Chisholm's "Service is the rent we pay for the privilege of living on this earth" and Marian Wright Edelman's "Service is the very purpose of life and not something you do in your spare time."[2] We hear these sayings and sentiments in church pews, in community center halls, and in our own kitchens.

Those who receive opportunities and never make those same opportunities available to others in the community lose respect. Alice Walker, in her poem "For My Sister Molly Who in the Fifties," describes the daughter who goes away to college, reads much, learns much, and picks up "accents never heard / in Eatonton"; the family is in awe of Molly because she is the one "who found another world"—a world beyond her provincial upbringing. But the poem announces that Molly "*left us*" (emphasis added). As I mention in the essay "Smarts," "The poem does not fault Molly because her education took her to many different places; it faults her because she did not know how to travel to those places and still travel home again."[3] The desire to reach back, come back, and pay back has always been at the forefront of what some would call responsible citizenship and engagement in the Black community.[4]

Even so, other African American faculty hear the communal voice more as an intrusion on their personal rights, subtracting from them time that their white colleagues are not asked to surrender. In a "First Person" column from the October 12, 2007 *Chronicle of Higher Education,* an assistant African American professor bemoans the pressure placed on him to attend campus Kwanzaa celebrations, Martin Luther King breakfast celebrations, and Black commencement celebrations.[5] The essay describes how "pressured to be seen at certain college events, a black professor decides to redefine his role on campus." At some point most African American professors ask themselves the question that this professor raises in his essay: what do the pouring of libations, the speaking of Swahili, and the beating of drums have to do with the advancement of my academic career? The professor relents and attends his campus version of a Black graduation ceremony, and it does turn out to be, as he describes it, a "bizarre performance," helping him to recognize that he does not want to assume that type of Blackness:

> That bizarre performance led to a decision. I would attend no more kente-cloth breakfasts. I would not attend a Kwanzaa celebration. Never again would I applaud speeches that celebrated the myth of black defeat, and I would not participate in events simply because of the color of my skin. And if people questioned my absence, I would not tell them a lie.
>
> I intend to be visible, I would tell them, but only in ways I wish to be seen.[6]

For some, service to one's home community, whether on or off campus, is a distraction; for others, such as African American Professor of Family Studies April L. Few,[7] service is what she feels she must do to "nurture the soul," "to provide voice to the values [she] holds," and to maintain a commitment to social justice and activist pedagogy.[8] Few's essay, jointly written with her chair of tenure and promotion and her department chair, argues that academe's conceptions of scholarship should be broadened and offers to tenure-track faculty of color ten recommendations that include such motivational advice as "Do not give up who you are. Live your commitments, your passion. Be strategic. Fit your commitment for service into your research and teaching."[9] The previously mentioned *Chronicle of Higher Education* essay and the essay in the *NWSA Journal,* where the Few article was published, demonstrate the ends of the spectrum—African American faculty who resent how their presence is always already racialized and those on a mission to "deconstruct which [institutional] values should matter."[10]

Many misunderstand why African American faculty are complicit in their own service enslavement, not realizing that African American cultural beliefs, literature, and folklore shape a service ethic that makes it difficult to say no.

How does one determine which work is more important and what constitutes too much work? In African American folklore there are many jokes about mules who did not want to work because they were not the ones defining and evaluating "work." There are many variations of these folk jokes, but they all center on how much work a mule (read: the Black underclass; the marginalized; those in the lowest ranks) is supposed to do. One such joke describes a white man who cannot get his mule to work, so he asks a Black farmer to help him. Confident, the Black farmer tells the white man that he can definitely get the mule to work. The Black farmer has a way with mules. One variation of the joke has the conversation running along these lines:

BLACK FARMER: Watch me get this ole mule working. Okay, [*turning to the mule*], Obadiah, start working.

[*The mule does not move*].

BLACK FARMER: Okay, Zechariah, start working.

[*The mule does not move*].

BLACK FARMER: Okay, Zephaniah, start working.

[*The mule does not move*]. BLACK FARMER: [*turning to white man*] Now watch the mule start working *this time*. Malachi, start working.

All of a sudden, the mule starts working.

WHITE MAN: If you knew his name was Malachi all along, why did you call him by all those other names?

BLACK FARMER: I couldn't let that ole mule think he was the only one working.

The joke is playing upon the stereotype that Black people do not want to work. It is a stereotype that has been particularly troubling because of its roots in the slave economy. Throughout the tales of ex-slaves, the slaves complain that no matter how hard they work, no matter how much cotton they pick, their masters think they are lazy.

Other mule stories decry how much work mules are expected to do. A variation of this tale is called "The Talkin Mule" tale.[11] An "ole feller" wants to sleep late, so he sends his son to fetch the mule, Ole Bill, and get the day's work started. The son runs into trouble because the mule does not want to start working. Ole Bill rolls his eyes, and after the boy keeps pressuring him to work, Ole Bill says, "'Evah mawnin it's 'Come round, Bill! Come round, Bill!' Don hahdly git no res fo it's 'Come round, Bill!'" Needless to say, the boy is shocked that the mule is talking. He runs home, shares the news with his "ole man," but his father accuses him of telling lies. The father tells his "ole lady" that he is going to get to the bottom of this, and with his dog, "Lil fice," running behind him, he goes to see the mule. Again, the mule complains every morning about having to work: "Evah mawnin, it's 'Come round, Bill!'" The "ole man" runs back to share the shocking news with his wife:

Ole man say to de ole lady, 'Dat boy ain lyin. He telling da troof. Dat mule is talking. I ain nevah heard a mule talk befo.'

[*The dog*], Lil fice say, 'Me neither.'

If mules (and dogs) could truly speak on behalf of themselves, then what constitutes labor would have to be reconfigured.[12]

In addition to African American folklore, work issues also figure prominently in African American women's literature, and voices from the community pass judgment on its worth. Zora Neale Hurston's "Sweat" describes the life of Delia Jones, a washwoman with a "great hamper in the bedroom," which she uses to sort white folks' soiled clothing to the dismay of her philandering husband, Sykes. Doing white folks' laundry for over fifteen years has paid for Delia's horse and house, items that Sykes wants to take from her and give to his mistress. Readers sympathize with Delia's hardwork ethic, her "knotty, muscled limbs, her harsh knuckly hands."[13] Sykes, an abusive husband, dismisses Delia's work ethic as being too Christian and too white. The other men in the community, however, denigrate Sykes for his choice of a mistress and for his lack of understanding that honest labor helps the community and raises Delia's stature in their eyes.

Community is central to the story. The men sit around on their porches and talk about how they treat their wives, how they define beauty, and what they think of housing a snake in the home. It is the community's conversation that drives and clarifies the narrative, and the reader must listen to the community, for its folk sayings and jokes shape how readers are to judge the characters. Delia's religious values and the folk talk on the porch condemn Sykes's behavior. Hurston's characters often find themselves in situations where voices from the community comment on whether they are working too much or not enough. In a reference to "Sweat," critic John Lowe points out that "the appearance of the communal comic chorus in the personages of the loiterers on Joe Clarke's porch constitutes another significant development in Hurston's craft." [14] When the community speaks in Hurston's narratives, they assume judgmental roles. The story ends with Sykes placing a rattlesnake in the hamper so it can kill Delia, but in a case of situational irony, the snake crawls in their bed and is there when Sykes jumps in. Delia knows that the snake will kill Sykes and watches his final moments but does not help.

The pull of the community's voice is strong, and many African American faculty want to respect that voice. For some, it is a matter of what is at stake by saying no. Who can afford to say no and to whom? When the community calls, it is not easy to "Just say no." Mildred, the maid in Alice Childress's *Like One of the Family: Conversations from a Domestic's Life* (1956) says yes when her girlfriend, Marge, wants her to do community activities and says no when her white employer wants her to refrain from doing so. The whole time that Mildred is working in the white folks' homes, she is spending her few hours outside of work politically engaged in Jim Crow issues, "Negro History" events, independence issues for African countries, and so forth. One of Mildred's white women employees, Mrs. B., disapproves of Mildred spending time reading "the colored newspaper" and worries that Mildred might be planning to attend a Paul Robeson concert advertised in the paper. Knowing that the employer thinks of Robeson as a radical race man, Mildred tries to avoid responding to the question about her activities outside of work; however, Mrs. B. insists on warning about how these community events can bring trouble to Mildred, presumably the loss of her job. Exasperated, Mildred tells Mrs. B. a lengthy story that begins with an old slave master and his slave Jim. The tale is an allegory of all of Black history with the master exploiting Jim through every era, ending with the master vowing never to let Jim's children profit from the 1954 *Brown v. Board of Education* Supreme Court case. Mildred uses the tale of historical and ongoing discrimination to announce that going to see Robeson is a task that is more important than cleaning Mrs. B's house. Rattled by the story, Mrs. B. does what Mildred tried to do when first asked about attending a Paul Robeson event: Mrs. B. changes the subject to a more neutral topic: "Yes, it sure is a nice sunshiny day, and I hope it doesn't rain." [15]

Alice Childress uses Mildred to show how presumptuous it is on the part of the white employer to pit the value of the community event against the need to maintain one's employment—employment controlled by masters and mistresses. Toni Morrison, too, has a story that vexes the relationship between the labor of the marginalized and the expectations of the privileged.

In Morrison's *Sula*, Hannah, yearning for what she views as the normalcy of nuclear family life, asks her eccentric, sassy, and economically poor mother, Eva, about "quality time." The mother responds by describing how she took good care of Hannah and her siblings, Pearl and Plum, under the worst of circumstances. Not satisfied with this response, Hannah retorts, "I know you fed us and all. I was talking' 'bout something else. Like. Like. Playing' with us. Did you ever, you know, play with us?"[16] Eva responds, "Play? Wasn't nobody playin' in 1895. Just 'cause you got it good now you think it was always this good? 1895 was a killer, girl. Things was bad. Niggers was dying like flies."[17] Eva keeps working, and Hannah keeps pressing her for an adequate response. Given their poverty-stricken status, Eva calls Hannah a "snake-eyed ungrateful hussy" for expecting her to go "leapin' 'round that little old room playin' with youngins with three beets to [her] name."[18] Eva, who never wanted to engage in this conversation in the first place, details all that she did to help her children survive. She responds to her daughter's need for play by asking, "Pearl was shittin' worms and I was supposed to play rang-around-the-rosie?"[19] Eva is arguing that her position in life shapes her philosophy of labor and love. Pain places pressure on play. Aesthetics tug against mere survival. Eva's response is a rawer rendering of the voice in Gwendolyn Brooks's "kitchenette building," where a poor couple bemoans that "'Dream' makes a giddy sound, not strong / Like 'rent,' 'feeding a wife,' 'satisfying a man.' For the poor, the poem argues, dreams must fight onion fumes. Therefore, the speaker dares not take too long mulling over the relationship between the aesthetic and the mundane, for if she is to take care of her personal needs, she would do better to listen for the flushing sound of the shared bathroom toilet: "Since Number Five is out of the bathroom now, / We think of lukewarm water, hope to get in it." [20] Those who live in kitchenette buildings must attend to the physical before spending too long contemplating the philosophical. As do all faculty, African American faculty want to advance in the academy. But how does one get faculty of color to be cautious about their service obligations without being dismissive of their home communities? In addition to whatever aesthetic project the scholar may be doing, these communities want a return on their emotional and spiritual investment. Who can afford "to play rang-around-the-rosie" if "Pearl was shittin' worms?" If the community is still under siege, if more males of college age are in jail than in the college classroom, if the disparity in healthcare, housing, and job opportunities remains unacceptable, then how is it that the scholar can afford to do only that work that will give himself or herself tenure? Again, a Gwendolyn Brooks poem advises to "First Fight, then Fiddle." The sonnet ends with the couplet, "For having first to civilize a space / Wherein to play your violin with grace."[21] Perhaps the time has come in the academy when faculty of color should not have to choose between fiddling and fighting.

Even as all faculty members must choose how to balance their lives and will be held accountable for doing so, the solution to the problem of too many service responsibilities for faculty of color can only partly be solved by ourselves. One solution rests on the shoulders of academe. Why not hire clusters, cohorts, cadres of faculty so that individual faculty of color can choose to be invisible, visible, or hypervisible? Why not initiate what the ADE Ad Hoc committee on the Status of African Americans Faculty Members in English calls "affirmative activism"?[22] Affirmative activism calls for action steps on the part of chairs and their undergraduate and graduate program coordinators, hiring committees, and leadership at the highest levels. Collectively, the action steps seek to change the climate in which faculty and students of color are expected to thrive. Some of the suggestions are calls for aggressive action: "Identify targets of opportunity instead of always waiting for candidates to surface in a national pool; start building curriculum and scholarly strength in African American literature and culture, whether or not your department already has African American faculty members in place and whether or not African American faculty members you may hire will be specialists in that area." Some of the suggestions are calls for equitable action: "Assign new course preparations to African American junior faculty members in the same proportion as to other junior faculty members, even when they have been hired to develop a new curricular area." And some of the suggestions are calls for a redistribution of priorities and resources: "Reallocate internal resources to create 'topping off' fellowships for graduate students from underrepresented groups, as is commonly done in senior faculty searches or for hires in highly competitive fields." The essay proceeds with detailing close to fifty suggestions that in the end would help alleviate a problem that the academy helped to create: the numbers of faculty of color are so few that they are not allowed to have a range of professorial identities. Without a critical mass, faculty of color will always be more constrained by service commitments than their peers.

I would like to think that as a product of a home community that expects its scholars to be willing to advise the Black Student Union, attend the rally for the latest political injustice, speak at the local Black bookstore about the Black Arts Movement, explain Toni Morrison's work to the Black women's local reading groups, and so forth, my attitude about service is more expansive than that of many of my colleagues. As a chair, I have been caught between protecting all of my junior faculty from service tasks while giving greater recognition to the various types of service that my senior faculty do. I have added "Community Building" as a new heading on the Annual Activity Report, allowing my colleagues to define community and name any activity that they can justifiably argue enriches their professional or work/life career. To give service value, it needs to be in the reward structure, and faculty must have the kinds of teaching workloads that allow service to inform teaching, as well as all three informing each other.

At the same time that many more women are chairing departments, I believe that the job has become more difficult, given uncooperative state legislatures, corporate models of funding of higher education, litigious students and faculty, the pressure to be entrepreneurial, the never-ending quest to advance beyond one's benchmark and affinity schools, and so forth. When my colleagues see me working late at night, they sympathetically ask me to give up something. "Go home, you do not have to do all that you do," they advise. So, I sit and ponder which university committee I should stop chairing: the University Diversity Council, or the University Compensation Committee for Faculty Governance? Do I step down from major committees just when I have the power and authority to make structural changes? Or, perhaps, which lecture should I not do—the one for the Women's Leadership panel? The lecture for the common text written by an African author? Or, which program review can I afford not to do? Which Department of English is doing so well with diversifying its curriculum, faculty, and graduate student body that I need not worry about adding my voice to the critique? Or, which department should I say no to when asked if I will be an external reader for a promotion to full case—certainly, not the case of the candidate whose field is African American literature, with a focus on race, gender, and sexuality? If I say no, then how many full professors are there who do precisely this work at a comparable school? Is the group that I am in large enough that I can say no to several of the cases and remain the kind of mentor that I choose to be for the next generation? Or, which summer institute do I say no to—the one for recruiting more underrepresented students to graduate programs in English?[23] The one for recruiting more underrepresented students to graduate programs in the arts and humanities?[24] The Summer Research Opportunities Program at the consortium level?[25] How should I calibrate, weigh, or measure these many demands? As Few mentions, one must be "strategic about the kinds of service" that one takes on,[26] as well as creative in using service as a handmaiden for one's scholarship. For my own calibrations, I subtract the amount of "reach back" that my home community asks of me from the amount of "fall back" that they have given to me throughout the years and continue to give. That is, when asked to speak at yet another Martin Luther King Jr. Day celebration, I subtract from my effort all the times when I was at a loss to finish the next book chapter and the church sisters prayed and fasted on my behalf. Many of these women, these othermothers, are like the mother in Alice Walker's poem "Women" who "knew what we must know / without knowing a page / of it / themselves."[27] I subtract from whatever perceived burden that the "reach back" costs those times, when, weary of writing the dissertation, I found encouragement in the question asked curiously but supportively every time that I returned home: "What degree are you working on *now*?" I subtract the burden of having to read their poorly written poems from their pride when introducing me as "Dr. Valerie Lee, PhD." Every time I tried to explain the redundancy of their titling of me, I heard them repeat, "But we haven't called you out of your name."

There is no denying that I am among the generation of African American scholars very much influenced by what Marilyn Mobley McKenzie describes as those who inherited the legacy of "lifting while we climb," those with "a cultural orientation to service."[28] As McKenzie so astutely observes, "When a black woman has a predisposition to serve, an activist sensibility to make a difference, and a heightened sense of responsibility to marginalized communities of which she is a part, she is particularly vulnerable to expectations that she will contribute over and above what is expected of others and that she will do the service that others have elected not to do."[29] In the early 1990s, I collaborated with seven other African American faculty and professional staff members under the collective name of "Andrea" to write about humanizing academic service. The essay details how as Third World women we felt that we were working a third shift—the graveyard shift.

But even so, we saw ourselves creating a third space, a space we created for "humanizing change." Looking back over a decade, I still affirm our final words in that essay: "Sweet grass baskets woven with our voices hold a collection of third-space ideas. We go to work. *We are Andrea.* At the day's end we remain Third World women living in a third space working a third shift. But we have learned that working the third shift has one irrevocable advantage: we are awake while others sleep, and in that wakefulness, we safeguard dreams."[30]

Granted, I do have a sense of mission that is affecting how I see my own politics of labor. Early in my career I attended a women's studies conference,

"Transforming the Academy," and I have never given up that project. Indeed, as a full professor at a Research I institution, chairing one of the nation's largest departments of English during the time when the Modern Language Association is calling for a "more capacious conception of scholarship," serving under a dean and under an executive dean who are both African Americans in identity and scholarship, and currently presiding over ADE, I feel more like the position of the biblical Esther: "Who knows that thou art come to the kingdom at such a time as this?"[31]

There are times when I wistfully sit back and imagine what it would be like to have a professional life where my ethnicity and gender do not place added demands on me. After all, the work that needs to be done inside and outside the academy should be a shared enterprise, especially among feminist scholars. Mobley McKenzie pinpoints part of my worry: "When our fellow women scholars can analyze race in texts but shy away from doing so in everyday life interactions outside of the texts they study, we have a tangible manifestation of the politics of labor."[32] Can I trust those who are interested in racial discourse to hear the community's call and to understand that intellectual work need not stop at the campus gate?

In determining when to say yes and when to say no, I weigh how I want the climate of my return visits to the community to be. I choose not to return as Gloria Naylor's Reema's boy, who with his technology in hand returns home to do "extensive fieldwork," but his academic notion of fieldwork falls short of how his community defines work in the fields: Reema's boy "aint never picked a boll of cotton or head of lettuce in his life."[33] I choose not to return as Dee in Alice Walker's "Everyday Use," parading the new relationships that I have formed, the new words acquired, and the new foods eaten—then arguing that she needs to take with her some of her grandmother's quilts, apt symbols of folkness, to decorate her walls. Her fear is that her sister who did not receive a college education, would "be backward enough to put [the quilts] to everyday use."[34] I choose not to return as the college-educated young people in Toni Cade Bambara's "My Man Bovanne," who exploit "the folks" as grassroots specimens for their political agendas. As someone for whom social justice is still an important cause, I choose not to return as someone "playing rang-around-the-rosie when Pearl is shittin' worms."

Underground Railroads on Postracial Tracks?

The task of Critical Race Theory is to remind its readers how deeply issues of racial ideology and power continue to matter in American Life.—KIMBERLÉ CRENSHAW

Many Critical writers are postmoderns, who believe that form and substance are closely connected. Accordingly, they have been using biography and autobiography, stories and counter-stories to expose the false necessity and unintentional irony of much current civil rights law and scholarship.—RICHARD DELGADO

Because of their historical grounding and literary feats of imagination, neo-slave narratives are more popular than ever. In his introduction to the Beacon Press edition of Octavia Butler's *Kindred*, Robert Crossley accurately describes the neo-slave narrative's genre dilemma, noting that the end of American slavery did not end the future of the genre as one might have expected:

> The American Slave narrative is a literary form whose historical boundaries are firmly marked. While first-person narratives about oppression and exclusion will persist as long as racism persists, slave narratives ceased to be written when the last American citizen who had lived under institutionalized slavery died. The only way in which a new slave-memoir could be written is if someone were able to travel into the past, become a slave, and return to tell the story. Because the laws of physics, such as we know them,

preclude traveling backwards in time, such a book would have to be a hybrid of autobiographical narrative and scientific fantasy. That is exactly the sort of book Octavia Butler imagined when she wrote *Kindred*, first published in 1979. Like all good works of fiction, it lies like the truth.[1]

As a literary genre, slave narratives, rather than dying out, are living a richer life than ever before, especially in the hands of African American women writers penning a range of imaginative retellings.

There is a sense in which much of contemporary African American literature is an extension of the conventions of slave narratives. Accordingly, scholars have examined how many twentieth-century African American texts revive/revise the structural, rhetorical, and thematic frameworks of slave narratives. One can readily find scholarship on how such works as Richard Wright's *Black Boy*, Ralph Ellison's *Invisible Man*, and Alex Haley's *The Autobiography of Malcolm X* participate in the conventions of the slave narrative. As autobiography, the historical slave narratives "had become a mode of Afro-American scripture"[2] and as such, like the Bible, the historical narratives have generated many contemporary translations/versions.

The versions that interest me are not texts that merely use the formulaic conventions of the historical slave narratives but texts that resituate themselves in the eighteenth or nineteenth century, use first-person narration, and are essentially new slave narratives—or to use the term that Bernard Bell coined, "neoslave narratives."[3] With Ishmael Reed's *Flight to Canada* (1976), Charles Johnson's *Middle Passage* (1990), Edward P. Jones's *The Known World* (2003), James McBride's *The Good Lord Bird*, and Colson Whitehead's *The Underground Railroad* (2016) as notable exceptions, many of these neo-slave narratives are by women writers. An early precursor of the present movement is Margaret Walker's folk epic, *Jubliee* (1967).[4] Since the publication of *Jubilee*, other African American women writers have written neo-slave narratives that are more experimental than Walker's: Octavia Butler's *Kindred* (1979), Sherley Anne Williams's *Dessa Rose* (1986), Toni Morrison's *Beloved* (1987), J. California Cooper's *family* (1991), Jewell Gomez's *The Gilda Stories* (1991), Michelle Cliff's *Free Enterprise* (1993), and Dolen Perkins-Valdez's *Wench* (2010). I am struck by the way these aforementioned texts speak to one another and am impressed by their range as neo-slave narratives: from Walker's folk epic to Butler's science fiction text, from Cooper's and Morrison's postmodern narratives to Gomez's Black lesbian vampire utopian fiction. What is there about the slave narrative that invites such diverse appropriation?

And why the renewed and gendered interest at this point in our nation's history? The fields of critical race theory and critical race feminism provide a lens through which we can examine why feminist neo-slave narratives are flourishing at this moment in history.

Before exploring the question through the two aforementioned critical lenses, let me dispel some misconceptions that might immediately come to mind. Misconception#1: Maybe slave narratives did not have an audience the first time around? Of course they did. Charles T. Davis and Henry Louis Gates's *The Slave Narrative* reminds us that the narratives had "an appreciable market" with Douglass's *Narrative* selling "5,000 copies in the first four months of publication. Between 1845 and 1847, the *Narrative* sold 11,000 copies; in Great Britain, nine editions were printed in these two years. And by 1860, 30,000 copies had sold." Davis and Gates proceed to give the successful numbers for other narratives, including Solomon Northrup's twenty-seven thousand copies within the first two years, Moses Roper's ten editions within an eleven-year period, and so forth.[5]

Misconception #2: Nineteenth-century women were not gender conscious. Of course they were. As Harriet Jacobs/Linda Brent declares in *Incidents in the Life of a Slave Girl*, "Slavery is terrible for men but it is far more terrible for women, given the mortifications that are peculiarly their own."[6] Jacobs and other slave women were conscious of their roles as women and made decisions that considered their lives as mothers, domestic servants, and slave mistresses.

If slave narratives have always had an audience, and if many of the narratives were gendered, what is it that contemporary women writers who are revisiting and reinvesting in the genre hope to accomplish? The early narratives assumed that the more knowledge one had of the horrors of slavery, the more likely people—especially white northern women—would help the cause of freedom. But today's writers make no overt appeals to white audiences. If anything, they critique whiteness as an "invisible norm in the West, a transparent, yet ubiquitous frame of reference so pervasive that even today most whites consider themselves absolved from race matters."[7] Rather than appeal to white audiences for compassion or support, these neo-slave narratives theorize whiteness and the law as partners in crime.

In *Playing in the Dark*, Toni Morrison raises the issue of the difference it has made that "the readers of virtually all of American fiction have been positioned as white."[8] The authors of neo-slave narratives use a genre that was definitely pitched to a white audience and rewrite the genre in such a way that their narratives become analytic studies of whiteness, doing the work that scholar Elizabeth Ellsworth calls for educators to do in her essay, "Double Binds of Whiteness"—work that moves beyond the identity politics of whiteness to analyzing whiteness "as a practice; a form of property; a performance; a constantly shifting location upon complex maps of social, economic, and political power; a form of consciousness; a form of ignorance; a privilege."⁹ As such, these slave narratives perform the work that many critical white theorists are calling for: the outing of whiteness by ending the silence on whiteness. Just as the earlier slave narratives were very much a part of the abolitionist movement fighting the laws of the land, I contend that these neo-slave narratives are very much a part of a "new abolitionist movement,"¹⁰ recontextualizing history by rewriting and unearthing historical legal cases.

To analyze the neo-slave narratives in tandem with the legal cases that they invoke is to invite a discourse about nationhood. Whatever reasons the early writers had for wanting to right the wrongs of the nation, the contemporary writers see the business as unfinished and are giving us texts that prompt dialogues about nationhood, Americanness, whiteness, and the totalizing presence of law in African American life. The neo-slave narratives revisit old terrain because the politics of America's racial and gendered landscape still needs pruning, but this time around the authors use the sharp shears of critical race issues to write stories that have their genesis in legal cases.

Such is the situation with the narrative *Dessa Rose,* based on the true case of a slave woman who led a slave rebellion and was kept alive long enough to give birth to her master's property. The white scholar in *Dessa Rose* is Adam Nehemiah, who interviews an imprisoned Dessa with hopes of learning what makes this "darky" tick. Thinking himself an expert on slaves since the publication of his work, *The Masters' Complete Guide to Dealing with Slaves and Other Dependents,* Adam is writing a sequel on the roots of slave rebellions and is trying to extract information from Dessa Rose, whose life has shown that "the female of the species is as deadly as the male."¹¹ However, Dessa, in a very convincing role as female trickster, does not give him the kind of linear information he wants. With much circularity she keeps speaking metaphorically and lovingly about her Black male lover and husband, Kaine, a discussion that Adam thinks is tangential to the text he is writing. For Dessa, Kaine represents sunshine and laughter. Their relationship was an act of rebellion against the system of slavery.

Adam, in his archetypal role as the first Adam, purports to name and define history. He is sure that his version of history will be accurate and full. *Dessa Rose* is a narrative that very consciously asks questions about the validity and multiplicity of historical interpretations. The reader hears two versions of what is supposed to be Dessa's story, one version as Adam Nehemiah sees her and the other version as she sees herself. Therefore, the larger issue within the text is the interpretation of history. Deborah McDowell notes that

> implied in the different versions of Dessa's story are a series of questions connected to the network of sociohistorical realities and power asymmetries that influence the manner and matter of representing slavery. Who has been publicly authorized or self-authorized to tell the story? Under what circumstances? What has been acceptably sayable about that story? How have black women been figured in it or figured themselves in it?[12]

Eventually, the community of slaves helps Dessa to escape, and she ends up on the land of a Miss Rufel, a white woman who nurses Dessa's baby, forms a loving and sexual relationship with one of Dessa's male slave friends (much to Dessa's disgust), and helps Dessa escape from the hands of Adam Nehemiah, a man who never gives up his search to find her. As the novel ends, Adam's historical notes get all mixed up, and his plan to get the local sheriff to look under Dessa's dress (the history "writ about her privates") fails. Dessa was supposed to be the subject of Adam Nehemiah's scholarly project. Obviously, he was not going to produce what one might call emancipatory research. Therefore, it is fitting that by the novel's end, Dessa, instead of calling him "Nehemiah," calls him the abbreviated and feminized "Nemi"; in other words, she has emasculated him. Neo-slave narratives veer away from stock portraits of cruel redneck overseers and concentrate on scholars, teachers, historians, lawyers—the role that learning and education played in enslavement.

As with *Dessa Rose, Beloved* distinguishes itself from the earlier nineteenth-century narratives by concentrating on white scholars instead of overseers or masters, similarly fleshing out the role that learning, education, and science played in slavery. Morrison bases her story on the historical account of a Cincinnati woman, Margaret Garner, who kills her child rather than have the child returned to slavery. In Morrison's novel, the dead child, Beloved, returns to haunt the mother. Morrison's version centers around Sethe, who escapes from slavery while eight months pregnant. While escaping, she gives birth, helped by a poor wandering white girl who is on her way to Boston looking for velvet. Although each begins the relationship distrustful of the other, they end up working together and doing it appropriately and well.

Sethe is free for eighteen years before schoolteacher and his sadistic nephews, who take breast milk from a pregnant Sethe, find her. When she sees the white scholar, schoolteacher, coming to recapture her, she kills her baby girl, Beloved, and attempts to kill her other three children. Racism for schoolteacher has been a scholarly pursuit, and Sethe would rather see her children dead than in the hands of this scholar who could "dirty you so bad you couldn't like yourself anymore. Dirty you so bad you forgot who you were and couldn't think it up. And though she and others lived through and got over it, she could never let it happen to her own."[13] One of the things that I see Morrison doing in rewriting the legal case is dealing with how whiteness is woven into the fabric of American society. Critical race theorist George Lipsitz argues that American society has a "possessive investment in whiteness" and that "white Americans are encouraged to invest in whiteness; to remain true to an identity that provides resources, power, and opportunity."[14] Theoretical in ways that the nineteenth-century narratives often are not, the neo-slave narratives unpack whiteness and "Americanization"—the transformation of groups from their individual ethnic identities to a deceptive amalgamation that has come to be identified as white. As James Baldwin notes, "No one was white before he/she came to America. It took generations and a vast amount of coercion, before this became a white country." [15]

Critical race theorists subvert or extend the traditional definitions of legal concepts. Take, for instance, the concept of "property." Legal race theorist Cheryl Harris posits that "because the system of slavery was contingent on and conflated with racial identity, it became crucial to be 'white,' to be identified as white, to have the property of being white. Whiteness was the characteristic, the attribute, the property of free human beings.[16] Harris is among an increasing body of theorists whose arguments go beyond discussions of whites as property owners to whiteness as owned property. Lipsitz reinforces that "whiteness is invested in, like property, but it is also a means of accumulating property and keeping it from others. While one can possess one's investments, one can also be possessed by them. I contend that the artificial construction of whiteness almost always comes to possess white people themselves unless they develop antiracist identities, unless they disinvest and divest themselves of their investment in white supremacy."[17] The African American women authors constantly return to notions of property, validating Jon-Christian Suggs's claim that "race in America itself is always already a narrative of property."[18] In Dessa Rose, Dessa faults the white woman character for "trusting in her whiteness and not our blackness."[19] Whiteness becomes an untrustworthy commodity. Morrison, too, challenges concepts of property throughout *Beloved*, and especially in the scene when the slave, Sixo, is accused of stealing property:

> "Did you steal that shoat? You stole that shoat." Schoolteacher was quiet but firm, like he was just going through the motions—not expecting an answer that mattered. Sixo sat there, not even getting up to plead or deny. He just sat there, the streak-of-lean in his hand, the gristle clustered in the tin plate like gemstones—rough, unpolished, but loot nevertheless.
>
> "You stole that shoat, didn't you?"
>
> "No. Sir." said Sixo, but he had the decency to keep his eyes on the meat.
>
> "You telling me you didn't steal it, and I'm looking right at you?" "No, sir. I didn't steal it."
>
> Schoolteacher smiled. "Did you kill it?"
>
> "Yes, sir. I killed it."
>
> "Did you butcher it?"
>
> "Yes, sir."
>
> "Did you cook it?"
>
> "Yes, sir."
>
> "Well, then. Did you eat it?"
>
> "Yes, sir. I sure did."
>
> "And you telling me that's not stealing?"
>
> "No, sir. It ain't."
>
> "What is it then?"
>
> "Improving your property, sir."
>
> "What?"
>
> "Sixo plant rye to give the high piece a better chance. Sixo take and feed the soil, give you more crop. Sixo take and feed Sixo give you more work."
>
> Clever, but schoolteacher beat him anyway to show him that definitions belonged to the definers—not the defined.[20]

This is as fine an example as any of a fiction writer theorizing human power relationships. With schoolteacher's observation, this neo-slave narrative returns full circle to the observation that frames Frederick Douglass's narrative: "You remember the old fable of 'The Man and the Lion,' where the lion complained that he should not be so misrepresented 'when the lion wrote history.' I am glad the time has come when the 'lions write history.' We have been left long enough to gather the character of slavery from the involuntary evidence of the masters."[21]

One would think that it would be hard to miss in Morrison's fiction her indictment of the domination of whiteness in political, social, and academic affairs. And for those who do, a reading of her essays unveils her continuing interests in legal definitions, court cases, Supreme Court appointments, and reparations.[22] Although of interest to departments of English as a fiction writer, Morrison is often overlooked for her overtly political writings. She has edited books on two major legal cases: Anita Hill and Clarence Thomas in *Race-ing Justice, En-gendering Power: Essays on Anita Hill, Clarence Thomas, and the Construction of Social Reality* (1992), and *Birth of a Nation'hood: Gaze, Script, and Spectacle in the O.J. Simpson or "Dead Man Golfing"* (1997). Morrison's interest in the law and the interest of other African American women writers in the law invite the use of a critical race theoretical framework, specifically a critical Black feminist framing.

What I see the neo-slave narratives doing in fictional form is akin to what critical white theorists and critical race theorists do in essay or argumentative form. And here I have a long list of recent books in mind: Noel Ignatiev's *How the Irish Became White*; Ian López's *White by Law*; Karen Brodkin's *How Jews Became White Folks and What That Says about Race in America*; Ruth Frankenberg's *Displacing Whiteness*; Richard Delgado's *Critical White Studies*; Michelle Fine's *Off White*; Theodore Allen's *The Invention of the White Race*, where Allen argues that when the first Africans arrived in Virginia in 1619, there were no white people. There were people who look like the Anglo-Americans of today, but they were not conscious of themselves as a race; Allen examines the transformation of English, Scottish, Irish, other European colonists from their various statuses as servants, tenants, planters, and merchants into a single new all-inclusive status: that of whites.

Jon-Christian Suggs points out in *Whispered Consolations: Law and Narrative in African American Life* that unlike white American literature that "reserves a genre category or two for stories grounded in the law ... classical African American literature is universally grounded in the law; in fact, all African American fiction carries the question of the legal status of blacks as its subtext."[23] That contemporary African American women novelists are overtly and passionately continuing a tradition of narratives grounded in the law speaks to unsettled issues. Legal theorist Thomas Ross notes that today we discredit Plessey and the other 19th century cases on race. Yet the rhetorical themes of the last century are still essential themes in our contemporary rhetoric of race, both within and outside the domain of law. The contemporary battles are over school busing and affirmative action, not fugitive slave laws and apartheid laws, but those who reject the remedies of busing and affirmative action also insist on the innocence of the contemporary white person and often use the device of abstraction to do so. Although the precise rhetorical structures are different, the central theme of white innocence and the use of abstraction to obscure reality run through the tapestry of our legal and social rhetoric of race, then and now.[24]

Needless to say, there is ample proof inside and outside of the narratives that these fiction writers see themselves as writing a past that is entangled in contemporary racial politics. In these narratives and in the essays by these contemporary women authors, they critique the continuing issues of who can write whose story, how caste and colorism divide Black communities, and the sexual politics of race relations. Critical race theorists read law and power in terms of narrative, a narrative of power. As Richard Delgado explains,

> Critical Race Theory's challenge to racial oppression and the status quo sometimes takes the form of storytelling, in which writers analyze the myths, presuppositions, and received wisdoms that make up the common culture about race and that invariably render blacks and other minorities one-down. Starting from the premise that a culture constructs social reality in ways that promote its own self-interest (or that of elite groups), these scholars set out to construct a different reality. Our social world, with its rules, practices, and assignments of prestige and power, is not fixed; rather, we construct it with words, stories, and silence.[25]

Similarly, in *The Alchemy of Race and Rights: Diary of a Law Professor*, Patricia Williams asserts: "I am trying to create a genre of legal writing to fill the gaps of traditional legal scholarship. I would like to write in such a way that reveals the intersubjectivity of legal constructions, that forces the reader both to participate in the construction of meaning and be conscious of that process. . . . To this end, I exploit all sorts of literary devices, including parody, parable, and poetry."[26] Although mainstream legal studies is not enamored with the use of parable, allegory, and myth as political discourse or a way to arrive at truth, critical race theory and its most recent offshoot, critical race feminism, do not hesitate to use literary devices to discuss the dynamics of racialized and gendered power in an attempt to answer the same questions that feminist neo-slave narratives raise: Who is a citizen? Who is free? Why and how do dominant narratives colonize Black women? What impossible ethical situations have Black women been asked to face?

All these questions permeate Octavia Butler's *Kindred*. *Kindred* begins in Los Angeles in the bicentennial year of 1976 with Dana, a twenty-six-year-old Black woman living with her white husband Kevin. Suddenly, Dana becomes dizzy and finds herself on a riverbank in antebellum Maryland. At the river, she saves a white child, Rufus, from drowning. When Rufus's father sees Dana, he plans to shoot her. At this very moment, Dana is inexplicably zapped back to the present. After several other rescue missions that take Dana from the present to the past, she begins to understand that her mission in life is to save Rufus, a rather wild child, from premature death until he and a slave woman, Alice, can conceive a child, Hagar, who will begin Dana's own family line. Dana must accommodate herself to slave society, something her white husband who accompanies her on one of her trips back in time is able to do much more easily than she could have. After completing her mission, Dana leaves the antebellum South mutilated: "I lost an arm on my last trip home."[27] Needless to say, Butler is stretching the boundaries of the historical slave narrative, whether one looks at *Kindred* as science fiction or what Butler calls a "grim fantasy." Other authors write neo-slave narratives that are full of postmodern ironies. In J. California Cooper's *Family*, the slave mother, while trying to poison herself and her children, dies while all of her children live. However, the mother's death early in the narrative does not keep her from watching over her living daughter, Always, or from narrating the rest of the novel. All the narrative surprises make for a reading of slave narratives that is not unlike the way Sophoclean audiences confronted the various Oedipus stories. They knew how the stories must end but not what the actions would mean to Oedipus. With the neo-slave narratives, today's audiences know that the stories will deal with identity, history, oppression, survival, but not what any of these topics will mean to Dessa, Sethe, Dana, Gilda, and Always. Given the vantage point of history, readers know the meta story, but they cannot predict how the writers will spin their individual tales or weave the complexities of their craft.

In *Neo-Slave Narratives* critic Ashraf Rushdy posits that the authors of neo-slave narratives struggle over "the costs and presumptions involved in a modern author's adopting the voice of a fugitive slave and employing the literary form of the antebellum slave narrative. Most important, [these authors] ask what it means for a postmodern author to negotiate and reconstruct what is essentially a premodern form, one in which 'race' was both a presupposition of authenticity for the author and yet a necessary absence for the primary white northern readership."[28] When contemporary African American women writers recast history, when they "redefine the way we narrate the slave experience," do they go too far? Are the neo-slave narratives deconstructing themselves through narrative and fantastical manners—with a baby ghost "who sits at the table as commonly as cornflakes for breakfast";[29] with slave women whose textual bodies thwart white scholarship, narrate from the grave, go back in history paradoxically to avenge and save the lives of rapist masters; with John Brown talking to Malcolm X; or with abolitionists who are lesbian vampires? Have the neo-slave narratives gone too far? Can you park an underground railroad at a postmodern terminal without losing passengers and without raising the cost of the ticket?

Historical slave narratives are classic texts cut from the cloth of unspeakable things unspoken. In giving us new slave narratives, are contemporary women authors stretching the seams of the garment, or are they, as I imagine, giving us new fabric, tie-dyed in recent political movements and tighter than the original?

"Forty Devils Can't Make Me Obey You"

Dinah, a slave, is badly beaten after allegedly sending word to a white man, Lovett, who had ordered the delivery of several dresses from her that "she would not send the dresses until she had got them done, and that forty devils and the defendant himself could not make her send them until she got ready." Lovett gave Dinah "a severe whipping, with a cow-hide, and . . . kicking her in the abdomen, and knocking out one of her teeth, and other-wise beating . . . commenced in the public streets . . . and was continued in the kitchen of defendant . . . (who) was aided by two other negroes, one . . . ordered to take hold of Dinah's feet, and the other . . . of her head . . . the physician's bill . . . was about fifty dollars, . . . verdict for the defendant."[1]

The case of *Johnson v. Lovett* came before the court by the plaintiff Johnson on an "action of trespass" against the defendant Lovett. Enslaved African women rebelled in many ways, short of fleeing north. Such is the case of Dinah, whose mouth got her in trouble. Dinah took pride in her work as a seamstress. Much like how one sublets property, she was hired out by her owner, a man named Wiggins, to a man named Johnson. Johnson let Lovett use Dinah's dressmaking skills. When Lovett pressed Dinah to hurry up and bring him the assigned dresses, she refused to do so before she had finished her work. She purportedly says that "forty devils and the defendant him-self" cannot make her deliver the dresses before meeting her own standard of excellence. Hearing that Dinah had given such a sassy answer, Lovett beat her badly, demanding the help of other slaves. Dinah was unable to work for another two weeks. Johnson was sent a physician's bill for fifty dollars, which he thought Lovett should pay. Lovett claimed that after two weeks, Dinah "seemed as sprightly as before" and assumed no responsibility for beating Dinah on a Sabbath Day in 1858. Although the court admitted the punishment to be "both indecent and excessive," no action was taken against Lovett, and Johnson was forced to pay the bill.

Although many details are missing from the original source, there is much to unpack about this case. Firstly, there is Dinah's voice, a voice that knows something about forty devils. In the Bible, forty is an important number. Examples abound: during the flood Noah spent forty days and forty nights in the Ark; the Israelites spent forty years traveling to the Promised Land; Moses sent spies to the land of Canaan for forty days; Jesus was in the wilderness for forty days and forty nights; and there were forty days between His resurrection and ascension. Perhaps Dinah had heard some of these biblical stories. She uses the "biblical forty" to tell her master that forty devils couldn't make her deliver goods before she was ready to do so. Massa becomes another devil, and Dinah dares to call him one. The events happen on what the case calls the "Sabbath Day," and Massa, rather than being God, becomes the forty-first devil—one devil too many for Dinah. Massa laboriously whips her, ignoring the admonition of Exodus 20: "Six days shalt thou labor and do all thy work, but the seventh day is the Sabbath of the Lord thy God. In it thou shalt not do any work, thou nor thou manservant, nor thou maidservant, nor thy cattle that is within thy gates." Because the case mentions that the actions took place on the Sabbath Day, I imagine that the intensity of the whipping and the solicitation of servants/slaves to help with the work might have violated the community's standards for keeping the Sabbath holy.

The case shifts, however, from Dinah's outcry and subsequent beating to the physician's bill. The cowhide whipping, kicks to the abdomen, knocked-out teeth, and bounding of her feet and head pale in importance to the cost of the physician's bill. After losing the case, plaintiff Johnson did try unsuccessfully for a new trial on the basis that another servant/slave said that Dinah did not truly send such a sassy message. This hearsay communication from another Black person was not accepted as a valid declaration. Dinah is a foremother to the many Black women who have mumbled under their breath or loudly proclaimed that their labor demands respect. As with Dinah, these cries have been heard from public streets to private kitchens.

Woods v. Green (Ohio 1834)

This case involves two horses that looked similar. One horse belonged to Woods, a white man, and the other horse belonged to Green, a black woman. One horse "has been wounded ... in the breast, in the flank, under the belly ... and on the hip." When the black woman came to claim her horse, she has to prove that the healthy horse was hers. She described her horse as having "a habit of leering his ears," and also explained that he would "obey her call." She provided the court with a demonstration—"She spoke to him, called him Tom, ordered him into the stable, and he walked in ... The horse was then bridled and brought up to the fence, ... He held off from the fence— she reached up ... and spoke sharp to him to come up, and he instantly obeyed. ... Verdict for the defendant"[2]

The case of *Woods v. Green* is described in court records as a "replevin for a sorrel horse" case. Woods has a horse that a Black woman, Green, says belongs to her. To assume that Black women living in the nineteenth century did not win cases against white men is false. This woman living in Ohio in 1834 won a civil case for a return of property. When one owns so little, one tries to hold on to whatever property one can. Green had probably voiced that the horse in question was hers, and in order not to give her such horse, Woods brought the matter to court. Everyone in court was probably surprised by the way Green had developed a relationship with her horse, Tom. That relationship proved her point because the horse responded to all her commands. Naming a horse "Tom" strikes me as odd. Not "My Friend Flicka," or "Black Beauty," but "Tom," perhaps naming him after a lover or a son. To build relationships is a humanizing act, and Woods probably had not thought of Green in terms of relationship building, certainly not with horses. Woods was not a horse thief; she was a horse whisperer.

Hardy v. Voorhies, Sheriff (Louisiana, August 1859)

Modeste, a pregnant slave, was found guilty by a "special tribunal," and sentenced to be hanged fifteen days after the birth of her child. Over a year elapsed and Modeste did not give birth, and therefore could not be put to death because the conditions of the execution had not been fulfilled. The District Judge ruled that the Sheriff should proceed with the execution. This ruling, however, was overturned because the District Court "was without jurisdiction" (676). It was suggested that the State "apply either to the Governor or to the Justices who had presided for the purpose of having a day fixed for the execution."[3]

In *Hardy v. Voorhies, Sheriff*, Modeste is accused and found guilty of murdering her mistress. There has been no delay in hanging her alleged accomplice, Joseph. However, Modeste is with child. It was not uncommon for pregnant slaves who were scheduled to be hanged to have the hanging delayed until after the birth of their child. Infant Black babies were valuable property. Sherley Anne Williams's *Dessa Rose* is based on such an incident of a slave woman's execution delayed until the birth of her child. Modeste is a mockingly paradoxical name for a slave, for modesty is an impossible virtue when one does not own one's body. Nevertheless, Modeste ensures that no one will own the body of her child. However powerless she might have been when appearing before the special tribunal, she proved to be an effective sistah conjurer. Faking and sustaining a twelve-month pregnancy are not easy feats. We have heard of the stories of slave mothers who have killed their children rather than have them live the life of a slave. To avoid her doom and tomb and the enslavement of her child, Modeste willed her child to stay in the womb.

Hawkins v. State (Missouri 1841)

Rebecca Hawkins was arrested and accused of the murder of her husband. Though told by Hawkins to remain silent, Mary, a "Negro woman" who helped her, refused to do so. Mary stated that "Yes, we all know about it; I shall have to die, and I am not going to tell any more lies about it." Mary went on to explain the details of the crime, including the fact that Hawkins gave her orders to put ratsbane in Mr. Hawkins' coffee. While it was initially thought that "the court erred in permitting what the negro said to be given in evidence," the court decided that "this rule cannot be carried so far as to exclude the conversation of a negro with a white person, when the conversation on the part of the negro is merely given in evidence as an inducement and in illustration of what was said by the white person."[4]

The case of *Hawkins v. State* begins by describing how Rebecca Hawkins was arrested at the burial of her husband who had died drinking poisoned coffee. At the time of the poisoning there were only two persons in the room, Mrs. Hawkins and Mary, a "Negro woman." Mrs. Hawkins did not think that

Mary would reveal what happened because to do so would implicate both of them. But Mary tells everything, including the names of others that Mrs. Hawkins had sent for the poison. Refusing to be quiet, Mary vowed not to "tell any more lies about it." She then proceeds to tell the court that if she is going to die, she will die telling the truth and not die protecting Mrs. Hawkins, whom she refers to as "Mistress." According to Mary, Mistress ordered her to place ratsbane in the coffee, and it was Mistress who then gave her husband the coffee. With this testimony, the court had what it needed to convict Mrs. Hawkins, who explained that she did what she did because of her husband's "ill treatment" of her. The problem, however, was that Mary, a Negro woman, could not testify against a white person: "It is contended that the court erred in permitting what the negro said to be given in evidence. That negroes cannot testify against white persons is clear; but this rule cannot be carried so far as to exclude the conversation of a negro with a white person, when the conversation on the part of the negro is merely given in evidence as an inducement and in illustration of what was said by the white person." Caught between a desire to convict Mrs. Hawkins of killing her abusive husband and the illegality of having a Black woman as the star witness, the court manufactured a loophole. Mary's voice was not really her voice. Mary was not *really* speaking. She was merely illustrating what the court heard her white mistress say. Mary did not own the words in her mouth.

Context is everything. Prior to taking my eldest daughter away to college, I had been reading hundreds of court cases of rebellious, sassy, womanish Black women slaves, servants, and would-be citizens. In the back of my mind, I thought that one day I would write a scholarly monograph full of such stories. Meanwhile, I was arming myself for the trip down south, imaging that my Midwestern-born daughter, like the women in my readings, would handle whatever came her way as she navigated her years at Oakwood University, a historically Black college in Huntsville, Alabama. As a professor myself, I vowed that I would not carry on crying like most parents who leave their students on the footsteps of a residence hall. Knowing that college would be the best years of my daughter's life, I sat through all the sessions for parents like someone anxious to get the show rolling. After all, I had built up fortitude through the readings of Black women in the worst of situations, and the only activity that my daughter had to do was study among her peers. Then, something very unexpected happened during this first-year orientation session.

On the eve of the last day that parents were in attendance, the college's president announced that there was a slave cemetery on the institution's grounds and that this cemetery was the burial place for the family of none other than Dred Scott. The president further stated that any parent who wanted to be a part of a sunrise service before leaving on the following morning was welcome to do so. The parent in me might have been dozing off a little during all the lectures, but the scholar in me immediately awakened to a wonderful opportunity. Only an HBCU would have thought of such an activity for orientation—descendants of slaves meeting at a slave cemetery to mark the launching of an educational milestone. The impact of such an event was not lost on me. Dred Scott had fought hard for his freedom, thinking that just because he had lived in several free states that he was free indeed. His fight for freedom ended with the Supreme Court (*Dred Scott v. Sandford*) ruling that property cannot bring a lawsuit before the court. Denied any recognition of personhood, not to mention citizenship, Dred Scott became a symbol of the struggle to claim one's rights. Indeed, Chief Justice Roger Taney asserted

Figure 7.1. Slave Cemetery. Stone marker leading to the Slave Cemetery, Oakwood University. Courtesy of Cheri Fisher Wilson.

Figure 7.2. Cemetery's Archway. Courtesy of Cheri Fisher Wilson.

the now-famous line that African Americans "had no rights which the white man was bound to respect."

Early the next morning, I convinced my daughter and husband to wake up and meet with others at the cemetery. If, as William Andrews says, the slave narratives are "a mode of Afro-American scripture,"[5] then slave cemeteries are sacred ground. I approached the stone marker and circular arch with reverence. A black dedicatory stone was placed on the site on April 4, 1999. The inscription reads: "This cemetery site was used as a burial ground for slaves who lived on both the Peter Blow and Job Key plantations from 1811 to 1865. Dred Scott's first wife and their two children are believed to have been buried here. The cemetery continued to be used through the early 1900s." Although Dred Scott was buried in St. Louis, that the remains of his family members might be where I was standing humbled me. I began walking among the headstones, noticing that most were inscribed with words from spirituals. In the morning light, these inscriptions captured the hopes of slaves in bondage, imagining a better day, if not in the immediate future then in a world to come: "Some O'Dese Mornin's Bright and fair/ I Thank God I'm Free at Las'

SLAVE CEMETERY
1800s

This cemetery site was used as a burial ground for slaves who lived on both the Peter Blow and Job Key plantations from 1811 to 1865. Dred Scott's first wife and their two children are believed to have been buried here. The cemetery continued to be used through the early 1900s.

Oakwood Historical Site

Figure 7.3. Dedicatory Stone connecting the cemetery to the family of Dred Scott. Courtesy of Cheri Fisher Wilson.

/ Gwineter Meet My Jesus in / De Middle of De Air, / I Thank God I'm Free At Las'"; "Deep River, My Home is Over Jordan." On another headstone were the words to *The Slave's Complaint*: "And When This Transient Life Shall End, / Oh, May Some Kind, Eternal Friend, / Bid Me From Servitude Ascend, / Forever!" Other headstones were inscribed with biblical scriptures or quotes from nineteenth-century writings on the equality of all peoples.

Given that reading factors so heavily in a liberal arts curriculum, what does it mean to start one's college years walking among headstones of dead slaves for whom it was against the law to read? How is first-year orientation, which at many institutions focuses on the mechanics of changing courses, meal plans, student organizations, and the etiquette of living with roommates, altered by a focus on freedom, resistance, and the presence of ancestors? How is the fight for justice, agency, and freedom a fitting frame for a liberal arts education? The cemetery visit was so jarring that when I revisited the college for Alumni Weekend, I again was drawn to the slave cemetery. This time I had my sister, Patty, with me. It was Easter Sunday, and I was snapping pictures much too

Figure 7.4. In absence of names, the Negro spiritual, "Some O'Dese Mornin's" covers the headstone. The song promises freedom and deliverance. Courtesy of Cheri Fisher Wilson.

Figure 7.5. Popularized in contemporary times by the voices of Paul Robeson and Marian Anderson, "Deep River" is one of the more famous Negro spirituals and a fitting inscription to grace the headstone of slaves for whom crossing rivers represented freedom and salvation. Courtesy of Cheri Fisher Wilson.

long for Patty's patience. Finally, she confessed a fear of being in a cemetery on Easter Sunday—Resurrection Morning. "Dem bones, dem bones, dem dry bones" were not about to rise, but the spirit of all those men and women who dared to defy their masters and the law of the land was still rising.

In more recent years, Oakwood has decided to plant cotton and other crops on some of its unused acreage. Driving by the land, I saw the white fields and immediately asked my children to stop the car.

"Is that what I think it is?"

"It's cotton, Mommy," they all said in unison. Out of the car I jumped. Had I been reading Ralph Ellison's *Invisible Man* too many times where a wealthy white benefactor wants to get out of the car to explore the rarely seen parts of the surrounding areas of an Alabama HBCU? Years removed from when Ellison was writing, I am at another Alabama HBCU and a Black woman positively engaging with a history that this university, unlike Ellison's fictional university, sees no shame in displaying. The Black college president in Ellison's novel mercilessly chastises the student for taking the white benefactor/trustee to an area near campus where slave quarters remain. The president considers it the height of ignorance to expose the college's white benefactor to this type of history: "And here you are a junior in college! Why, the dumbest black bastard in the cotton patch knows that the only way to please a white man is to tell him a lie! What kind of education are you getting around here? Who really told you to take him out there?" he said.[6] Colleges still struggle with what parts of campus, what buildings, what side streets should be shown to visitors. I applaud those HBCUs that refuse to hide the history upon which they were founded. I am told that places such as Tuskegee (the college critics believe to be the model for the *Invisible Man* institution) now proudly show their incoming students the gravesites of university founder, Booker T. Washington and faculty member George Washington Carver. In fact, several HBCU institutions have historical reminders of their beginnings—not the statues of Confederate soldiers and politicians but relics that tell the narrative of people wanting to be free. So as soon as I saw the cotton fields, I had no qualms about jumping out of the car and coaxing my children to let me use the last two pictures on my pharmacy-bought camera (in the premobile smart phone camera era) to take a picture of me on the first cotton field I had ever been in.

Two years later, I would bring my twin sons to this HBCU to join their sisters, and again I insisted on partaking in the same rituals of going to the slave cemetery and walking through cotton fields. But I would soon learn that I was getting too comfortable with southern plantation life. In my sons' junior year, my husband and I agreed that they could live in an off-campus apartment. Oblivious to the cost of their tuition, our sons selected a luxury apartment. When I filled out the application form, I forgot that I was surrounded by cotton fields and inhabited by some who still thought that my sons should have been working those fields. When the young white woman behind the desk of the rental office read the lease application, she told me, "You don't make enough of an annual salary to sign on behalf of your sons." Stunned, I was looking outward at the pool where white college students were living in the same complex and wondering what they or their parents earned that could possibly qualify them to meet the minimum salary that I, as a full professor and administrator at a research university, could not meet. When the young lady told me that $20K a year was too low a salary, I politely but firmly told her that the $20K was my monthly and not my annual salary. With her mouth hanging open, she consulted with someone else who looked as young as she did and promptly asked for my human resources telephone number. At the end of the day, she had to give my sons the apartment. She was well aware that my husband, who was with me, was a lawyer, and sensed that I, feeling a kinship to the many slave women who dared to bring judgments against unfair institutions, was ready to sue the apartment complex.

Before my sons settled in, I reminded them that the surrounding cotton fields hid a history that they had sooner learn. Traveling south was always part southern romance and part intergenerational trauma. Cemeteries and cotton fields—both were sites of memory, unexpected parts of what I knew from freshman orientation at my PWI (predominately white institution). Where were the bands and cheerleaders, the big-city welcome, the ice cream socials? No, when I traveled to orientation at an HBCU, forty devils couldn't make me bypass the slave cemetery and cotton fields.

Cartoons That Saved My Administrative Life

For me, life in the academy has been fun: that is, whenever I snatched time from meetings, conferences, student advising, and teaching to breathe and reflect, I often found humor in much of what was going on, especially when I became an administrator. As one of my fellow chairs once told me about faculty in her department, "Everyone is a specific kind of crazy." There were times when I felt I had advanced from working with one group of crazies to the next. For comic relief, I kept an archive of cartoons from the *Chronicle of Higher Education* and the *New Yorker* in my desk drawer. When wondering why I took on a certain position, I would pull from that drawer a Stan Hunt cartoon of two men standing together, one a boss and the other his employee. The boss wraps his arm comfortingly around his newly advanced employee and says to the stupefied man, "I'm so pleased with the way you handled that lousy, thankless job I gave you, Frawley, that I'm going to give you another one."[1]

I identified with the feeling of moving from one challenging task to the next. My first job as a departmental chair at a large research university where many departments had well over fifty to eighty tenured and tenure-track faculty was chairing what some called a "boutique" department—the Department of Women's Studies, so called because of only fifteen well-placed faculty lines. Of course, most women's studies departments at the time envied the many tenure lines we had. Although I agreed to chair only after a national search did not yield our desired candidate, running a women's studies department [now women's, gender and sexuality studies] that large was a pleasurable interdisciplinary experience. But right in the middle of my term, when everything was going well, when our activist graduate students had finally called a truce with our theory-heavy professors, when our undergraduate students had finally grasped what we meant by service learning, and when the Board of Regents had approved our request for a doctoral track, well-meaning ambassadors showed up at my door to convince me that the point in chairing a boutique department was to gain the necessary experience to govern a large faculty department of sixty-plus, the Department of English. I was as stupefied as Frawley in the cartoon. Why would I want to write forty-five more annual reviews, review four times as many tenure cases, and divide limited pools of money among larger numbers of faculty and staff?

To help me see more clearly what was ahead in chairing the Department of English, one of the department's previous chairs (whom I greatly admired not only as a great chair but the best teacher of twentieth-century fiction that one could ever have), Professor Morris Beja, sent me a note attached to a cartoon that had been passed down to him when he was elected chair. His note simply said, "Valerie, what to expect, Maury." The *New Yorker* cartoon by Warren Miller is of a man rowing a boat while six other men sit on the other end with megaphones.[2] That is all there is to the cartoon, but it was enough for me to clearly decode a message:

- The chair is the person doing all the rowing. The faculty are giving directions loudly—with megaphones.
- The chair sees one landscape, the faculty another.
- The faculty still have clothes; the chair is wearing the bare minimum.
- The faculty are announcing their own agendas; the chair is navigating the sharks in the water.
- Q &A: How do you know that the professors in the canoe have the rank of full professor? They are all older, white men.
- Q & A: And what are you? A newly elected, newly minted full professor who is the first woman and faculty of color to chair the department. Hmmm...
- Q & A: Why are all the men in a canoe and not a motorized boat? Change is slow in the academy.

Of course, my feminist impulse was to keep several cartoons that satirized patriarchal influence throughout higher education. One such cartoon by Barbara Smaller depicts two white women talking about a white man who is sharing a couch with one of them. Referring to the man, one of the women says, "Larry is a white male, but he hasn't been able to do much with it."[3]

I came across the Smaller cartoon while I was team-teaching a Critical Race Narratives course with a professor of law. The class was reading philosopher Charles W. Mills's well-argued book *The Racial Contract* (1997), which discusses the "differential privileging of the whites as a group,"[4] a privileging whereby whites are beneficiaries of what Mills calls the "Racial Contract":

> Both globally and within particular nations, then, white people, Europeans and their descendants, continue to benefit from the Racial Contract, which creates a world in their cultural image, political states differentially favoring their interests, an economy structured around the racial exploitation of others, and a moral psychology (not just in whites but sometimes in non-whites also) skewed consciously or unconsciously toward privileging them, taking the status quo of differential racial entitlement as normatively legitimate, and not to be investigated further.[5]

After teaching Mills's highly textured arguments imagine me returning to my office and pulling out Smaller's simple translation: "Larry is a white male, but he hasn't been able to do much with it." The cartoon satirizes the longest beneficiaries of affirmative action: white men. When one's membership is in a group that has a long history of writing the rules, earning the most capital, owning the most land, and ruling the landscape, one is in a better position to thrive. Rather than being surprised at how few African American or Latinx faculty make it all the way to full professorship, or why students of color have lower retention rates than their white peers, academe should justly ask why those white males who flounder do so when they are the inheritors of so many benefits, privileges, and advantages. I recently visited a prestigious K–12 private school that has so many programs, technologies, and luxurious facilities that I remarked to the Board of Trustee Chair and the headmaster that I did not see how any of its graduates could possibly fail with so many entitlements. That response probably cost me a seat on its board.

Several of the cartoons in my archive are of animals making a case for diversity. Perhaps audiences are more open to what animals have to say than they are to what people have to say to each other. Typically, these cartoons have an animal of one species interrupting the social or professional life of animals of another species. In all these cartoons, the out-of-place animal is easy to spot, whether she is a female cat among male dogs, a fox among hens, or a duckling among swans. One such cartoon has a fish joining dogs at a bar. Another has a fur-bearing animal at a conference table with white men.[6] Both cartoons foreground inclusion and exclusion issues, as well as issues of representation, isolation, and power. When you are the first person of color or the first woman in any type of leadership role, you are hard pressed not to notice that you look different from others in the room. Underrepresented people can see that they are underrepresented. Overrepresented people assume that their presence is necessary, the norm, and take for granted that they will be at the table. They expect to eat and not be eaten—to be at the table but not on the menu. Often, when I served on committees that failed to hear my voice, I turned to these cartoons that challenge how difference circulates in closed circles. Despite my similarities with my colleagues, and because on a daily basis I was facing racism on micro and macro levels, I was the alien species.

Cartoons that have one animal that is perceived as invading another animal's kingdom helped me when doing diversity training for search committees. The lone animal who is entering the heretofore closed space should not have to be the search committee's diversity advocate or affirmative action officer. Everyone should take on that role, and if a specific assignment is to be made, why not choose one of those older-looking males (presumably full professors)? And why do so many of the committee members look alike? Overtly or unknowingly, they have been replicating themselves and not entering into any new alliances. It is clear in the cartoons that the animals do not cross species. Unfortunately, this has been the argument as to why some have opposed interracial marriages. One day when I was in my mid-twenties and single, a white male colleague of mine who was a few years older and also single shared with me a dream that he had. He said that in his dream he was dating all the single women in the department, but when the time came to date me, he hesitated because dating me would not be mere dating; it would be "mis-ce-ge-nation," carefully pronouncing each syllable. Young and not attracted to him, I quickly responded that he would *never* have to worry about me polluting his "nation." Years later, I would learn that he previously had dated a prominent Black woman critic.

Admittedly, some of the cartoons that I have kept in my drawer are not on the surface about race or gender, but through my lens they are raced and gendered. Charles Barsotti has a cartoon of a short white male in a suit standing behind a table facing a large rattlesnake wearing glasses and showing its teeth. The snake says to the man, "You've been warned, Hoskins."[7] As a Black woman senior administrator, I am perceived as the snake in the cartoon: hostile and angry. Before Michelle Obama settled down and started planting gardens, she was portrayed as angry. And Oprah is most loved when she is not playing the strong, raging Black woman that she played in the films *Native Son*, *The Color Purple*, *Beloved*, and *Selma*. Belonging to a group that has often been burdened with hostile and angry tropes rather than strong and powerful ones, I sometimes find it difficult being authoritative and respected, rather than falsely branded as overbearing. On the one hand when deciding who should get promoted, receive a merit increase, or be assigned additional duties, one cannot be a pushover. One has to be strong. But Black women are caught between an overwhelmingly strong caricature of themselves as bossy and the desirable skills of firmness, resoluteness, and transparency that characterize many good leaders. It would not be until I became vice provost for diversity and inclusion, a unit with many Black and Brown staff persons, that I could be sure when assuming a firm posture, I would not automatically be dismissed as hostile. But even in more multicultural spaces, there were still moments of questioning my leadership postures. When I first arrived in the building housing diversity and inclusion programming, one of my Black male directors greeted me, "Oh, so you are the new HNIC." On a predominately white campus, I was taken aback by hearing what I knew to be slang in Black communities for "head n----r in charge." This director suddenly noticed the puzzled look of my white administrative assistant who was in the room, prompting him to shorten his appellation to "IC"—in charge. Afterward, every time he saw me, he greeted me, "Hi, 'IC'" with enough warmth that my white staff members would think he was being respectful but with enough persistence to remind me from whence I came. Every time he said "IC," he knew that I heard the full greeting, "HNIC." Although half-amused by his brashness, I never detected hostility or anger in the greetings, just a mutual understanding of what the acronym signifies. Perhaps the most famous animal cartoon that resonates with my administrative career is of the dog sitting at a computer and telling another dog that "on the Internet, nobody knows you are a dog."[8] I have been searching for anonymity my whole academic career. That happens when one is underrepresented; you stick out and can never blend into the crowd. I recall an incident early in my career when some well-meaning feminist researchers were doing a project on women's bodies. They wanted to demonstrate how women's bodies are contested terrains and needed at least one female body of color. Their idea was to superimpose pictures of contemporary bodies on ancient paintings and sculptures. Of course, these scholars did not have the artistic skills and political imagination of a Kehinde

Wiley whose portrait paintings effectively install Black figures atop classical European noblemen, interrupting Old Master paradigms. When I received the call from the researchers, I listened intently until they got to the part that the painting would be Sandro Botticelli's *The Birth of Venus*. Yes, that is the painting of the goddess arising from a seashell, naked, with her long tresses discreetly covering her privates and a hand covering one breast. As my callers continued describing how they would not use my name and simply say the body was a woman colleague in our institution's consortium, I had already tuned out their voices. Having visited the Uffizi Gallery in Florence, Italy, and viewed the original painting, I did not need them to give me any more details. How could they promise anonymity to a Black woman professor who was the only Black woman professor at her university and one of two or three in the whole institutional consortium to which her university belonged? And as the youngest such professor at the time, I imagined that students would immediately know whose breasts and buttocks were on the screen. This project was my first emphatic "no" to a white feminist project.

Anonymity and hypervisibility have framed my life. During my very first sabbatical in the academy I listened as one of my white feminist friends shared with me some of the social and behavioral changes I should make while on sabbatical. She promised me that her advice would prove very useful. "Make sure you change all your bank checks to carry your husband's and your titles. You will get better service on airlines, at hotels, and even at the local IGA grocery store." I followed her advice, changing my checks to "Attorney James Lee & Dr. Valerie Lee." What a disaster. Frequently, store clerks would call their managers who would look me over as if I had stolen the checks. Because this was during the time when *The Cosby Show* was popular, clerks asked me over and over again, "Is your family the Cosby family or something?" I was as much a fiction to them as Cliff and Clair Huxtable. It is no wonder so many accomplished Black professionals suffer from the Imposter Syndrome; when questioned over and over again if you could possibly be the person your credentials say you are, you start to doubt yourself. Not wanting to overreact to every slight, my archive of cartoons was a needed distraction.

Even when I should have been meeting a necessary deadline, I sometimes lost time by looking at cartoons. Anyone keeping a full and complicated calendar can identify with a cartoon by Robert Mankoff of a man looking at his schedule and talking to someone on the phone. The caption reads, "No, Thursday's out, James. How about never—is never good for you?"[9] It is also a cartoon for those of us who do not want to set a date for a meeting with

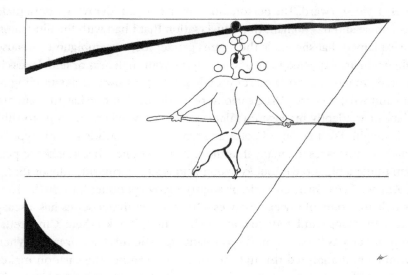

Figure 8.1. Angelia Lee, "On the Rope," in "Corporate Circus Life Series," 1970s.

the trustee who wants to raise the ACT/SAT scores every year, the helicopter parent who wants to discuss her child's essays, the community activist who has an idea as to how the university can help advance his business, or the student group leader who wants you to be the faculty adviser for the Reading in the Wilderness Student Association. When I was really busy, I would look at Mankoff's cartoon and enjoy the satisfaction of mentally giving the person the date of "Never," agreeing with poet Joy Harjo that "*never* is the most powerful word in the English language, or perhaps any language."[10]

As useful as these cartoons were for me as a source for keeping all my duties in perspective, I did wonder, "Where was the canon of cartoons by Black women who surely knew the need for comedic release?" Had anyone followed Jackie Ormes, the first Black female syndicated cartoon artist?[11] I did come across some cartoons by educator and artist Angelia Lee, whose illustrations speak directly to the quandary that sometimes I found myself in as a Black woman: Lee's "On the Rope" depicts a person juggling nine balls while walking on a tightrope and carrying a balance pole. It is a cartoon depicting funambulism, the technical term for tightrope walking, and is from Lee's series on what corporate life is like for people of color—a veritable circus. The person in the cartoon has been given a difficult task but is determined to delicately tiptoe forward. The person looks like a bodybuilder who is both male and female and has no hair. In a conversation that I had with the illustrator, Lee explained that she made the figure's gender identity ambiguous because "when you are expected to be a work engine your maleness or femaleness is ignored. You are absurdly out of proportion to your own understanding of who and what you are."[12] The cartoon reminds me that one has to maintain balance (or adeptly manage imbalances) and know when and how to shift one's weight. For persons of color and women in the academy, this type of funambulism leaves too many flummoxed because one is being asked to perform under a big top without knowing who is sitting ringside: ally or foe?

Angelia Lee's Girlfrien' series is a particularly apt outlet for visually contextualizing some of my experiences. One cartoon in her series has a scary little man asking Cinderetta to make up her mind, "Look-a-here, Cinderetta, I'm your Fairy G Person; now do you want me to do this trick or not?" When reframed and analyzed through my own background, the cartoon makes me think of how many of my colleagues who have marginalized status in the academy toy with whether they should go into administration, stay in administration, leave the academy, or press onward through the ranks of tenure and promotion. In the cartoon Cinderetta is looking outward toward the viewer, not knowing what to make of the academy's promises because the academy looks like it is in no condition to grant its own fantasies. The impatience of the Fairy G Person is baffling to a Cinderetta who already seems to be bringing more to the table than what a pumpkin can deliver. She does not know if she can trust Fairy G[odfather]. After all, he is asking her to trust the trick that the waving of a wand can make something happen as quickly as one can say "poof."

Another cartoon, "Hair Hang-ups" in Lee's Girlfrien' series illustrates the decisions that professional Black women have to make on a daily basis. The cartoon's caption notes that there are many choices for Black women who are always already mammies and sapphires. Interestingly, the cartoon presents the choices in an alphabetically alliterative way. Should Girlfrien' wear "braids, beads, barrettes or should she use "creams, conditioners, colors, curls, cut, corn-rows" or "weaves, waves, wigs," or finally, "headbands, hennas, hot combs, hairpins, . . . ha . . . HATS!" In the middle of what looks like a messy and confused boudoir, a Black arm reaches in and offers a hat. Yes, a hat would solve many problems, and in reintroducing a hat as the solution, the artist is returning the Black woman to the tradition of Black women wearing hats

Girlfrien'   by Angelia Lee

Figure 8.2. Angelia Lee, "Cinderetta" in Girlfrien' series, 1980s.

Look-a-here, Cinderetta, I'm your Fairy G Person; now do you want me to do this trick or not?

Girlfrien'   Angelia Lee

Figure 8.3. Angelia Lee, "Hair Hang-ups" in Girlfrien' series, 1980s.

Braids, beads, barrettes, creams, conditioners, colors, curls, cuts, corn-rows, weaves, waves, wigs, headbands, hennas, hot combs, hairpins, ...ha...HATS!

Figure 8.4.
Angelia Lee,
"Dr. Matters"
in Dr. Matters
series, July 2020.

to church, to funerals, to any event where they want to make a statement. Hats solve hair problems. Although I have seen a few of my colleagues don an Afro cap or a mud-cloth cloche, they are more likely to grab a headwrap and tie it with creativity and flair.

Cartoonist Lee's most recent series is her Dr. Matters series. Dr. Matters (as in "Black Lives Matter") is a professional woman. In my favorite Dr. Matters cartoon, Dr. Matters is a professor, "award-winning and renowned." She probably is a visiting guest lecturer because she is speaking in a large auditorium, and off to the side is another woman who probably introduced her to the audience. The topic that Dr. Matters speaks on is an ambitious, complex one: "the role of women in politics during the Middle Ages and at the same time across the Middle East and West Africa." She even shares some graphs for comparative data. When she finishes, the audience of what appears to be mostly white students clap, and the question-and-answer period begins. The very first question is: "Can I feel your hair?" When looking at this cartoon, I ask myself: at the end of the day, have I been chosen as the subject matter over the words leaving my mouth? Rather than unpacking my arguments, have my students been detangling my hair, undressing my body? No matter how erudite Dr. Matters's lecture is, what the students want is more knowledge of the texture of her hair. Granted, Dr. Matters seems to have more hair on her head than anyone else in the room, and her hairstyle looks more flamboyant than that of anyone else, but the question about hair trivializes and detracts from any substantive engagement of the subject matter.

A complementary cartoon is Lee's post-9/11 "Harassment Hair." As Dr. Matters walks through security at the airport, all the alarms go off. She definitely is not "Bold Derrick," a reference to the white actress, Bo Derek, who in a film entitled *10*, was celebrated as a perfect "ten" on beauty scales, rising out of the water with her hair in cornrows, a style associated with Black women but judged unprofessional and unattractive on Derek's contemporary Black actresses such as Cicely Tyson. Not seeing Dr. Matters as any type

Harassment Hair   Angelia Lee
Flying after 9/11 and not quite Bold Derrick wondering why she had to pay for her ticket after going through airport security.

WHAT A TRIP! And I haven't left the airport! OK, I know you thinking these clips on my braids belong to a gun and these are little ninja knives. My beads must fit into a mini cannon that doubles as a camera. If I sneeze its C-4 to 50 projectiles. But after getting patted and wand across my boobs for a wire bra, and up and down between my legs make me want to SCREAM, take a shower, have a drink, and a smoke —— UGH... FLYING!

Figure 8.5. Angelia Lee, "Harassment Hair" in Dr. Matters series, August 2020.

of Bo Derek, airport security feels compelled to check her hair. Disgruntled, Dr. Matters complains that the security guard must think she has hidden all kinds of weapons in her hair, not to mention the explosives that may be concealed elsewhere in her bodily parts. The other passengers wait patiently in line because they know that deweaponizing a Black body might take a long time. This cartoon resonates with me because every time I go through security at the airport, the guards insist on checking my braids/locs, a rather embarrassing act when accompanied by one's colleagues. This type of hair ritual at the airport helped me be more earnest when giving implicit bias workshops.

I cannot count how many workshops I have given on implicit biases. It has been difficult standing in front of STEM professors and explaining that we all have unconscious biases that war against even our best impulses and values. I imagine that some of them think that when people of color do such work, we are working solely from a self-interested platform, never imagining that the life to be saved may be their very own. One of the ways I broke the ice with my listeners who perhaps felt I was somehow accusing them of discriminatory impulses was to share how I, too, had to learn to confront implicit biases. One story that I often shared was when one of my colleagues in the English department came to me as chair to admit that he was the culprit running up costly telephone calls on his office phone after midnight. To make me believe how contrite he was, he felt compelled to share his personal story behind making such calls. As it turned out, he was having an affair with a woman at another university whose schedule in the theater department kept her unavailable until very late at night. Because cell phones were beginning to gain popularity, I asked him why he simply did not call his lover on his cell. His reply was that the cell phone in his home belonged to his wife. As I was watching him twitch in his chair, crying between explanations, I found myself caught in implicit biases. The whole time I was thinking, "How is it that this man who has so much to say at faculty meetings, who prides himself in being an astute theorist, can sit before me crying tears like a baby? Why doesn't he just 'man-up'"? I quickly controlled my thinking. Had the culprit been a woman colleague in a similar situation, I probably would have offered at least the kind of give-me-a-tissue and hug sympathy one finds in television's Hallmark romance movies.

Yes, we all have our implicit biases, but some biases are crazier than others and could easily be dispelled with more contact with each other. The current trend of weaponizing Black people's braids at airports is a follow-up to the way Afros were seen as instruments of violent protest. Simone Browne has a chapter in her book *Dark Matters: On the Surveillance of Blackness* (2015) that deals with the trouble that specifically Black women have with natural hair at airports. One of the stories that Browne shares is that of Solange Knowles, who after having her hair searched at the airport, exclaimed in a now-famous tweet, "My hair is not a storage drawer," inviting her millions of Twitter followers to guess what might be hidden in Black hair.[13] Ever since 9/11 with its deepened terrorist threat, I try never to walk with a white colleague through security checkpoints because of the embarrassment of having security check my hair—although when was the last time anyone heard of an African American woman hiding explosives in her braids?

From Soweto to Harlem, from the Antilles to Accra

ONE LONG BLUES SONG

For nine summers during the 1980s I taught in a South African Orientation Program (SAOP) that was designed to help South African students adjust to American college classroom styles and content. Prior to my teaching in SAOP the Africa I knew best was literary Africa, canonized and conveniently situated somewhere between Joseph Conrad's *Heart of Darkness* and Graham Greene's *The Heart of the Matter*. Later, with an increasing awareness of African American writers, I relocated Africa, placing it this time somewhere between Countee Cullen's poem "What is Africa to Me?" and Langston Hughes's poem "Afro-American Fragment."

Teaching a thousand Black South African students for almost a decade awakened in me the yearnings, the double consciousness of which Hughes speaks, of the two souls in W. E. B. Du Bois's *The Souls of Black Folk*. For an African American to stand before such a large number of Zulus and Xhosas is to confront one's hyphenated existence—an existence as both African and American. Even Mr. *Roots* himself, Alex Haley, found such a task humbling. In his July 16, 1972 *New York Times* essay, "My Furthest-Back Person—The African," Haley speaks of the time when he first stepped upon Gambian soil, noting that he felt "impure among the pure" and musing "how difficult it is for African-Americans to see large numbers of Africans without weeping." In *The Color Purple* Alice Walker, too, tries to capture the experience of an

African American who comes in contact with large numbers of Africans. Her character, Nettie, writes that she felt she was seeing Black for the first time and that there was something "magical, dazzling, luminous" about doing so. There is something discomforting, too. Teaching the South Africans was a reminder of my own displacement and my need to connect my fragmented existence with theirs. Over the years, the program provided a forum for making those connections easier.

Each year the South Africans attended an occasion at the Martin Luther King Center in Columbus, Ohio, where the two communities strengthened their bonds, exchanging gifts of dance and song—African Americans singing the Black South African anthem, "Nkosi Sikeleli Afrika" and Black South Africans singing, "Lift Every Voice and Sing," Black America's national anthem. I watched our Black power fist become their "Amandla" salute and heard words from our vocabulary, "minority" and "Third World," become in their lips "majority" and "developing world." Two communities, each fascinated with the existence and the survival of the other, demanded answers of each other. Right in the middle of a discussion of some aspect of American literature, the South African students would ask me what I thought of Michael Jackson's nose job or whether I thought MC Hammer, ("U Can't Touch This") is an African American griot. Their annual trip to the Ohio State Fair in Columbus raised other questions as they saw young African American males with portraits of Africa carved in their hairstyles but no real geographical knowledge of where these countries were located. My South African students noted the many African American teens wearing T-shirts printed with the words Martin, Malcolm, and Mandela and asked me questions as to whether I thought the young women saw the three men as one continuous stream in liberation's waters.

So much about the two communities seemed similar—the sense of time, the flair for style, the love of oratory, the folklore, the food, the fads, the faces. Yet so much appeared different. Sometimes while teaching the group of students, I fancied that I could pass for one of them. But a tongue that has only had Germanic and Romance languages rolling off it has trouble with the clicks of Xhosa and stumbles over difficult, non-Western consonant clusters. And although I know how to greet one in Zulu ("Sakubona"), I must confess my device for remembering this greeting is to think of Cher's former husband, Sonny Bono.

When I listen to their names (Ntopane Chiloane, Sibusiso Gcaba, Mziwndile Madikizela) and compare them with ours (Leroy Jones, Rufus

Smith, Shaneka Jackson), I know that more than the sound of drums has been lost. During the last summer I taught in the SAOP program, I wore a different African outfit each day: a global bridge at best, an American indulgence at worst. Their outfits on my body still feel like costumes. There are not enough yards of kente cloth and not enough sartorial splendor to cover cultural nakedness.

Part of the process of educating for a new South Africa involves Black South Africans learning from the failures and successes of African Americans, especially our attempt to overcome a caste system (which although never legalized as uniformly as theirs, has certainly been pervasive). Their remarks in class alerted me that they had carefully studied and continue to study our liberation movement. The part of my task I relished most as an African American professor in the program was the type of Ruth/Naomi reassurance I was able to give them: your struggle is my struggle, your victory is my victory, your people are my people. Perhaps the distance from Soweto to Harlem is just one long blues song.[1]

After the experience of teaching the South African students during the 1980s, I began traveling throughout the African diaspora. Traveling around Dodowa, southeast of Accra, Ghana, I could not help but notice how Christian values dominate the names of most of the commercial establishments: "If God Say Yes Beauty Salon," "Salvation Barbershop," "Kingdom Food Court," "By His Grace Rentals," "Thank You Jesus Tires," "King Jesus Motors," "King of Kings Electricals," "Master Plumbing Works," "God Is Great Sporting Shop," and "Glory Oil." Amid all this mercy and grace, I am still drawn back to centuries of enslavement. As an African American, whenever I travel to a place of colonial power or to a place that has been colonized, I carry with me the heavy baggage of the formerly enslaved. After my treks around Accra, I began a pilgrimage to Elmina Castle. Elmina Castle is a place where, despite the pristine whiteness of its outside structure, on the inside one can still see and smell the stench of blood on the walls. When my guide showed me the dungeon space where the Black women and girls were kept (directly under the floor where the white Dutch Reformed Christians worshipped), I could hear the spirituals that one day these enslaved African women would sing: "Go Down Moses," "Swing Low, Sweet Chariot," "Steal Away to Jesus," and "Wade in the Water." My walk through Elmina's "Door of No Return" remains the most haunting walk I have ever taken.

When I was young and traveling internationally, I do not remember being as conscious of race and gender as I am now. As I have aged, I have become so much more aware of how people in power exploit the Other and how racism, sexism, colorism, and any category of difference is exploited by those in power. I spent my sophomore year at a college in France. That summer, prior to beginning classes, I traveled throughout Europe with a group of Americans, visiting what seemed like mostly castles and cathedrals. There were only a few times that summer when on my grand European tour race and gender were major concerns. When boating to Venice, I was separated from my traveling companions—twenty white coed students, one African American man, and one Afro-British/Jamaican woman. I ended up in a gondola with Eastern Europeans, mostly men, who heard me yell in English to my classmates that I would rejoin them upon arrival. I was nervous on the gondola because the waters were choppy, and the Eastern Europeans kept looking at me, pointing to some black-inked pens they held up and saying a few words in English: "mother," "father," "black," "all over?" I finally understood what they were using the pens to ask me: "Are your mother and father black? Are you black all over?" My impulse was to be sarcastic, "No, I'm polka-dot in some places." However, I was not a swimmer and had read too many times the story of the biblical Jonah, who to stop the stormy seas was thrown overboard and eaten by a whale. I politely answered, "Yes, I am black all over." Everyone smiled and we safely disembarked. Aside from a few instances where my accent (and who knows what else) betrayed my identity, I traveled as any nineteen-year-old would—as a carefree American tourist. When visiting Switzerland's Zermatt, I do not remember wondering why more African Americans had not attempted to climb the world's highest mountains. The only thing I remember is taking a cable car to get a better view of the Matterhorn and carving my then-boyfriend's name in the ice. When visiting the Louvre, the thought that one day a Kehinde Wiley would come along and superimpose his brand of black-ness on classical artwork never crossed my mind. When visiting Mad King Ludwig's Linderhof and Neuschwanstein Bavarian palaces, although amazed by the display of wealth, I do not remember connecting extravagance to socio-political issues. When traveling as a nineteen-year-old, the only places that awakened my political and moral sensibilities were my visits to a concentration camp and to Rome's Colosseum. But now with age, the more I travel the more vexed I find myself becoming, annoying tour guides with questions about identity, nationhood, and accountability.

In the Caribbean, no sooner than I find myself sitting under a mango tree eating rice 'n' peas, I am drawn to the monuments of slavery. I want to see the places that the maroon societies of escaped slaves built. In Brazil, I insist on visiting Bahia, where I am told there are more people of African descent than any place outside the continent of Africa. Although interested in ecological tourism and the coastal landscapes, I want to see the African influences of Salvador, the capital city, where the first slaves of the Americas landed. In London, no sooner than I have seen the Prime Meridian at Greenwich, I look at the maritime splendor and remember the slave ships—so many pretty names: *Aurore, Adelaide, Esmeralda*; and names that extol virtues and peace: *Desire, Hope, Nightingale, The Rainbow*; and names that speak of spiritual solace: *Madre de Deus, Lord*, and *The Good Ship Jesus*, reportedly the first slave ship to reach North America.

In Brussels, I walk past the statue, *Manneken Pis*, of the little boy who reportedly extinguished a potential citywide fire by urinating on it. But this statue is not what is consuming my thoughts. Rather, it is how Belgium's Leopold pissed all over the Congo, not as a little boy but as a grown man: a king who wanted, as my tour guide explained, his own private playground. In Africa, I see the Ashanti gold and think of the coins that some of their people would be sold for on auction blocks in Louisiana. Would that I could block this racialized mental roaming as easily as my cell phone blocks robocall roaming.

I write this essay from my hotel room in the Bahamas. In such paradises there is always a Pompey Museum, a site where slaves were auctioned. In the Bahamas it is located on bustling Bay Street, near the famous Nassau Straw Market and a hotel, the British Colonial Hilton Nassau. Yesterday my husband James and I hired a driver to take us around the island. While driving, he showed us the mango and coconut trees, the sea grapes, and a "love vine" so powerful an aphrodisiac that his wife has begged him not to boil it as tea. The driver spoke intelligently about American politics, what it meant to Bahamians to see Barack Obama elected as America's first Black president, claiming "He's the president of Black people worldwide." I proudly divulged that when casting my vote for Obama, rather than going to my regular largely white polling place, I went downtown and stood in a long line so that I could be among a more diverse group of voters. With locs in my hair, kente cloth on my shoulders, and Morrison's *Beloved* in my hands, I crafted how I wanted to present myself in that historical moment. More at ease that he was driving Obama voters, our driver beamed and connected himself more fully to us. He spoke of having visited Chicago many times (but never when it was snowing) and of American football, industries, and its economic role in the world market. Realizing that I was dealing with an astute mind while watching the grand gated communities of superstars pass my view, I decided to nudge the conversation where it was inevitably going. Knowing of his interest in folklore (with the love vine story, he also talked of "sky juice"—a pineapple, gin, coconut, and sweet milk drink that he claimed would be the drink of a New Eden), I asked him why more Blacks do not scuba dive or snorkel or swim with the dolphins.

"We carry within us the memory of the Middle Passage. The sea is not our friend," he replied and promptly stopped the car.

The sea is not our friend. I thought about Toni Morrison's estimate of how many Black Africans never made it into slavery or died either as captives or on the slave ships—*sixty million or more.*[2] The sea is not our friend.

"Over there. You see that area. It's called 'Sacred Space: Women.' Come and see."

There on the tip of the southwestern part of the island I saw wood sculptures, long gray bark with blackened faces of women nestled in a silent community on a cliff overlooking the ocean. The place is called Clifton Pier, and this is where the slave ships docked—on the opposite side of the magical "Atlantis" playground where we were staying. Here on Clifton Pier was a true lost city, a city of displaced Africans, many of their bones dissolved with other ocean debris. Then, I spotted a bell high amid an Australian pine tree.

"Oh, every time a ship came in, someone would ring that bell up there," our driver explained. *For whom the bell tolls* took on a new meaning.

Some of my colleagues probably think that my mind wanders too easily to a colonial past and that I am one of those Black nationalists who see race in everything. I remember a group of Black students from my college days who were so caught up in campus racial incidents that when they saw a flyer posted in a building advertising a lecture on black holes, they took offense, thinking it was yet another sexual slur against the sexuality of Black bodies. They did not read the small print: Department of Astronomy. So, yes, I have considered that I should free myself from thinking about colonialism, but just when I begin to critique my propensity to see race and gender as fundamental issues, I visit a beach in Guadeloupe, and the only women who are topless are white women from France. I wonder what the Black Indigenous women, fully clothed and selling their wares on the beach, think of this display of haute couture. I recall a travel essay about the Caribbean Island of St. Barts where the journalist/tourist Alan Behr, a very good writer of travel memoirs, muses that "the secret of St. Barts is that you do not feel that post-colonial tension of other places in the Caribbean—those formed by the evil of slavery and where the local population still serves (sometimes resentfully) interlopers from afar." Just when I want to take Behr at his word, he adds, "Any woman wearing a bathing suit top betrayed poor fashion sense; among those who had the physique to pull it off, nudity was widely practiced."[3] I want to be gracious and think that Behr is truly including all women on St. Barts, at least all "who had the physique to pull it off," but I circle back to a preceding paragraph that talks about "pretty young women from France" who staff all the hotels. What happens when the exotic Other is the colonizer's daughter?

I continue to try to enjoy the marvels of a location while curtailing my thinking on race and gender justice. On a trip to South Africa, (a place I had spent time previously attending conferences and visiting various universities, including Fort Hare, the alma mater of many of the ANC leaders), I vowed to concentrate on the beauty of the landscape. Certainly, Cape Town is one of the most scenic cities in the world. But then something happened. Nelson Mandela died, and I was within walking distance of his Johannesburg home.

Here's the backstory:

On Thursday, December 5, resisting jet lag, I traveled past all the Western companies on the outskirts of "Jo'burg," and went directly to Freedom Park in Pretoria.[4] At Freedom Park I saw "The Wall of Names." Etched on it were the names of those who died in political struggles—not just the apartheid struggle but *every* political struggle in South Africa. I thought the South Africans were trying to be a little too inclusive. After all, of the seventy thousand names on the wall, the names most tourists want to see are the names of those who died in the 1960 Sharpeville Massacre and those who died "on the right side of history" in the liberation struggle against apartheid. I was having difficulty understanding the generosity of the wall—everyone's name was there, including those of Afrikaners who in my mind were undisputable criminals. My tour guide did his best to explain inclusivity and the Truth and Reconciliation Commission, but the whole time I was thinking, *How could twenty million Black people in a country of only two million white people consent to a policy that lets anyone who tells the truth about a crime deemed "political," be forgiven?* I'm all for forgiveness, but as someone who went to high school south of the Mason-Dixon in the late 1960s and attended college in the 1970s, I was more used to a gospel of social *justice*. My forgiveness was closer to the words of Martin Luther King Jr.: "We will not be satisfied until justice rolls down like waters and righteousness like a mighty steam." That's forgiveness with clear corrective actions. That's forgiveness with accountability. But then that night Mandela died, and the next two weeks for me would be what professors call a "teachable" moment.

I rose early the next morning in my Jo'burg hotel and found out that I could go with the crowd directly to Mandela's home. I didn't understand what kind of protocol would permit me, neither kin nor acquaintance, to arrive on the deceased's front lawn the very next morning, but I was assured that all would be welcomed. I went and heard all the cries and shouts of, "Tata Madiba!" How is it that I did not know that his beloved name was "Madiba"—not the British name given to him by a white schoolteacher but "Madiba" his home name? And then I learned that his middle name, Rolihlahla (meaning "tree" or "branch/bridge"), was prophetically given to him at birth. I have always been interested in African American naming patterns, for as Toni Morrison writes, "Names bear witness." Although this essay can't veer off to the politics of naming, the reader should find it no surprise that before I left South Africa, I attended a naming ceremony and was given my African name, "Lumka," which was Xhosa for "wisdom."

During the next two weeks I bought every South African newspaper I could find, visited the Apartheid Museum, and rode on Rovos Rail—a train that advertises itself as "the Pride of Africa" and during apartheid was for whites only. It was not my idea to travel on such a train. Despite its luxurious Victorian and Edwardian suites, the train ran on tracks that were parallel to the tracks of crowded all-Black trains. I visited Madiba's Soweto home that sits on the only street in the world where there are two Nobel Prize winners across from each other. Madiba's home is right across from Bishop Desmond Tutu's home. I went to many memorial celebrations in both Jo'berg and Cape Town and had the opportunity to sign the funeral guest books on behalf of the Office of Diversity and Inclusion and the Office of Outreach and Engagement.

Surrounded by mountains, festooned by palm trees, and hemmed in by both the Atlantic and Indian oceans, Cape Town is where I spent most of my time. I listened to every news broadcast and was amazed that rather than just giving the facts with a human-interest story occasionally thrown in (as with our American news), all of the broadcasts focused on interviewing anyone who had something to say about Madiba: and everyone, young and old, Black and white, victim and perpetrator, had something to say. As a professor of English, I found the value that the people placed on storytelling to be extraordinary. I was especially interested in the stories that Madiba's enemies shared. They spoke about how even as they fought against Madiba, they were in awe of him. He convinced them that "your freedom and my freedom cannot be separated." It's one thing when your friends describe you in messianic terms; it's altogether more riveting when your prison guards ask, "What manner of man is this?"

Although the jet lag on my return trip wiped me out for a good week, I have finally shrugged off the South African time zone. What I have not been able to shake off has been my visit to Robben Island. I cannot see myself ever returning there. I saw the hard-labor limestone quarry where the brightness of the sunlight damaged Madiba's eyes, making reading difficult, and where the dust of the stone filled his lungs, making breathing difficult. Yet Madiba and his other educated comrades/colleagues made this quarry their own university, surreptitiously teaching the hardened criminals to read and write—criminals who were treated better than Madiba and his ilk were. I saw copies of the kitchen menus where the Black prisoners were given food rations based on how light or dark their skin was. It would be seven years before Madiba would receive a piece of bread. As someone adamantly opposed to any kind of torture, I choose not to tell all that I learned at Robben Island. And although I took pictures outside of Madiba's cell, the experience of seeing where he spent twenty-some years of his life—a life of silence and isolation—returning not as an insane, vengeful tyrant but as the first democratic president of a new South Africa, answered all the questions that my tour guide tried to explain to me. In South Africa, inclusivity means declaring all eleven languages the official language. Inclusivity means placing all the symbolic colors on the flag. As vice provost for diversity and inclusion, the word "inclusion" does not roll off my tongue as easily as it once did. I can't think of inclusion without thinking of Madiba, and I can't think of Madiba without thinking of dignity, respect, freedom, and yes, forgiveness.

Forgiveness is difficult, especially when one's visits to sites of trauma occur at propitious moments, having been in Ghana during its fifty-years-of-independence celebrations and in South Africa when Nelson Mandela died. My real test of forgiveness will happen when I have had a chance to visit the memorial to lynching victims at the National Memorial for Peace and Justice that first opened in April 2018. As described by *Washington Post* writer Philip Kennicott, this "monument to pain" located in Montgomery, Alabama, is "a somber hilltop pergola of rusted steel overlooking the city that saw the birth of both the Confederacy and the civil-rights moment [and] is one of the most powerful and effective new memorials created in a generation."[5] Because this monument has over eight hundred coffin-shaped boxes hanging from a ceiling and jars with the names, dates, and soil from where lynched bodies fell—now that my own body has weathered storms—this might be the site that I struggle between wanting to see and hear the honesty of histories and the need to keep some pains at bay. It is the struggle between believing legendary Black feminist Audre Lorde's pronouncement that "your silences will not protect you" and award-winning Black journalist Michele Norris's acknowledgment of "the grace of silence"—that one of the reasons why her ancestors and parents did not allow their trauma from racial slights show in front of their children was because "you can't keep your eye on the prize if your sight is clouded by tears. How can you soar if you're freighted down by the anger of your ancestors?"[6] It has gotten difficult to discern whether I want to see more or experience less. Globetrotting while Black, daughters of the diaspora carry baggage too heavy, too full of hazardous material, and too large to fit in white, male overhead spaces.

Retirement

NO MORE MONDAY MORNINGS

I started watching soap operas while working on my master's degree. I had a roommate from Bermuda who watched *All My Children* and *General Hospital* on those days when we were not in our Nathaniel Hawthorne seminar. There was always more going on at Pine Valley and Port Charles than there was at the House of the Seven Gables. As far as our Shakespeare seminar was concerned, *General Hospital*'s Luke Spencer (Anthony Geary) and Laura Webber (Genie Francis) made Romeo and Juliet seem like third graders pulling off the petals of daisies: "She loves me; she loves me not." Many years after graduate school I gave birth to my first child on the day that Luke and Laura were getting married. Not wanting to name my daughter Laura, I selected "Erica" in homage to *All My Children*'s vixen Erica Kane, the woman whose list of husbands was almost as long as the number of years she had to wait to win an Emmy: Erica Martin, Brent, Cudahay, Chandler, Montgomery, Montgomery (again), Chandler (again), Marick, Marick (again), Montgomery (again). (I think I left out Roy?) I never told my husband where the idea to name our daughter Erica came from.

When I retired, I found out that soap operas were worse than I had remembered them being. Because *All My Children* had ended its run, I decided to check out what was happening on *The Young and Restless*, a soap I had occasionally watched. Firstly, the only people I still recognized were the villains. Only Victor Newman (Eric Braeden) looked the same; the other family members were either new or had aged. Even though I was now in my sixties, I was surprised to see that Melody Scott Thomas, who plays Nikki Newman, was turning sixty years old. I was still watching through the lens of graduate school memories and was a bit taken aback by all the new young actors and the aging of the actors who I thought were immortal. Watching the soaps drained my mental peace. Although on the surface an Erica Kane might seem close to a Becky Sharp, *All My Children* and the other soaps never brought the pleasure that reading Thackeray's *Vanity Fair* did: there were too many babies switched at birth; too many corporate takeovers; too many storms forcing wives to take shelter in the wrong arms; too many people experiencing amnesia or coming back from the dead; too many people receiving kidney donations from their worst enemies; too many lovers finding out they are in incestuous relationships. Watching the soaps became more stressful than chairing a department of English, calming women's studies graduate students, or managing diversity initiatives in STEM. The soap actors slept around more than the most active undergraduate students, lied more often than strategic action plans, and delivered more tours de force than state legislative funding.

Rather than filling the vacuum left by soap operas with the novels that I promised I would reread (or, read for the first time, in the case of lengthy blockbusters *War and Peace* and *Middlemarch*), I started binging on Hallmark Channel romance movies. Quite the opposite of soap operas, these stories are chaste—no one kisses a lover until the very last scene, no bedroom antics among married or unmarried partners, no adultery, no fornication—only rural white girls who leave their bucolic small towns and flee to a large city, only to return to their blueberry farms or family campsite lodges where there is peace, purpose, and a prince. Sometimes, the young lady meets a real prince. Indeed, I have never seen so many middle-class women who are able to attract the fancy of royalty as in these Hallmark romances. The weddings are always predestined and the outcomes restful and not stressful. Although these movies were relaxing to watch during times when I tired of partisan news and crime movies, I found Hallmark's attempts at adding diversity to its casts a bit incredulous. The best friend of the white woman is usually Black or biracial, the all-white towns happen to have Black mayors, or the noble prince has a Black caretaker who manages his life. The movies remind me too much of an additive approach to diversity, a first step but not the end goal. To truly diversify requires some transformational changing of the template: small, isolated towns often are scary sites for the marginalized; winter won-derlands where skiing is the sport of choice are not where one finds crowds of tourists of color. Moreover, why would any Black person want to be the only person of color in a town? Where are the other family members? So, given the raunchiness of soap operas and naiveté of Hallmark romance movies, when the call came to return to my university and chair what would be my third department, I said "yes." I worked another two years and then decided that enough was enough—no more free speech debates, oversight committees, TED talks and podcasts, 360-degree evaluations, assessment rubrics, hiring colleagues, or appeasing clueless administrators. Although this may sound like I have grown tired of academe, I do know that there is no other life I would have desired except life in the academy. I feel privileged to have had such a job. Internally, I remain that little girl whose mother used a cardboard box to cut out the letters of the alphabet, giving them to me to play with while she ironed clothes. The first word I ever spelled on my own was "FAB," a soap detergent that my mother was using at the time. Every grade that I was in was the grade that I announced I would teach when I grew up. Each grade seemed to be the ideal grade. It is little wonder that I ended up becoming a college professor, teaching mostly graduate courses.

Approximately seven months after retiring, I was honored and humbled to receive several distinguished service awards, a coveted one bestowed at a commencement service from my home university, and on its heels, one from my professional organization: the Modern Language Association's Association of Departments of English (ADE) Francis Andrew March Award. An expanded version of my acceptance speech would later appear in the *ADE Bulletin*:

RECLAIMING, REFRAMING, AND REIMAGING SERVICE:
A CAREER IN RETROSPECT

My Foremothers and Labor:

My grandmother, Lydia Bell (known as "Ma Bell"), was a domestic for a wealthy white family in Greenwich, Connecticut, though her own ten children lived in Maryland. As I often have mentioned to my students when reading a novel with a Black domestic character, "someone's mammy is someone else's mother." Ma Bell took pride in the fact that her Greenwich *charges* (dare I say, "children") obeyed her, more so than they obeyed their own parents. Although attentive to the Greenwich household children, Ma Bell was never as accommodating as the domestic in *The Help* who tells the little white girl, "You is kind … you is smart. You is important."[1] Ma Bell had too strong of a Black consciousness to feel the need to reassure white children that the world was theirs to claim. Nevertheless, she worked hard and pleased the Greenwich family so well that when she returned to Maryland, still strong and in her seventies, the Greenwich family promised her that they would send her a generous monetary birthday gift until the day she died. Ma Bell died three months shy of her 101st birthday. The Greenwich family kept their promise.

My mother lived her childhood in a home where her grandmother, my great-grandmother, Annie Mason, reigned supreme. Annie was the person who taught Ma Bell how to wring a chicken's neck, press sheets with a cast iron, wash clothes on a scrub board, and cook five different dishes from the yard's apple tree. Born two years after slavery ended, Annie Mason worked hard all her life. Whenever my grandmother and mother failed to live up to her expectations, Annie warned them that they "would never get a job in a white woman's kitchen." Given the limitations placed on Black women's labor, working "in a white woman's kitchen" was the marker by which my great-grandmother had learned to measure success.

Although Ma Bell had worked as a domestic, my mother, Ann, grew up to be a reader, a lover of words who now at eighty-five years old continues to play *Scrabble* against the computer, many nights until past midnight. Although I am the one who taught her how to play *Scrabble*, I am no longer able to win against this person who nightly beats the computer and has memorized the dictionary of two- and three-letter words and all the "Q-without-U" words. Working as a domestic was not the job my mother was seeking. During her career as an archives technician at the National Archives,[2] she too worked hard, performing a type of work very different from what Annie Mason or Ma Bell had done. My mother took extra steps to help researchers locate documents, earning accolades for cataloging historical papers and meticulously preserving national records. Growing up, whenever I hinted that I was going to shortcut work, I had to bear my mother's warning that all honest work is worth doing well. To support her position, she quoted maxims from the Bible, her foremothers, and a few I recall that were mouthed by Benjamin Franklin.

My Career and Service:

My foremothers empowered me to choose academic work as the type of labor I would do. As Annie Mason's great-granddaughter and Ma Bell's granddaughter, I entered the academy with a strong sense of the dignity of hard work, a work ethic born out of the need to feed and clothe their children.

Theirs was a dutiful labor. However, as my mother's daughter, I entered the academy equating service with pleasurable activities. I witnessed her pride in safeguarding historical documents and the gratitude she felt when visiting scholars, who always seemed to be working on their own manuscripts, acknowledged her in their books' prefaces.

Even during the early years of my career when I had four children four years old and under (two daughters and an unexpected set of twin sons),[3] I never saw myself as having to work any harder than family members before me. Indeed, compared with the manual toil of my great-grandmother and grandmother, I had it easy in many ways—summers off, presenting papers worldwide, choosing whatever novel I wanted to teach and on what days and times I wanted to teach it.

Of course, I soon realized that the path I had chosen was not without its challenges, including the isolation of having been the only tenured Black woman on campus for the first fifteen years of my career. Initially, not realizing that many of my colleagues would succeed by prioritizing teaching or research, or by claiming incompetence when it came to administrative tasks, I saw everything that I was doing—research, teaching, and service—as part of a whole, avoiding what Black feminists such as Toni Cade Bambara have called a "wasteful and dangerous split."[4] When publishers or readers suggested that Bambara departmentalize genres, mind/body, or psychic/political issues, she responded by writing a novel that would "fuse the seemingly separate frames of reference . . . identifying bridges."[5] For me, teaching, research, and service always have been interlocked, interdependent, and integrative.

Complementing my immediate family's emphases on labor, I am a product of a particular Black community whose folklore, literature, and popular culture address issues of labor: the many stories that Zora Neale Hurston wrote about labor (e.g., "Sweat") and the folktales she collected about mules/and Black people who question how and why they labor, as well as Hurston's Black women characters who see themselves the "mules of the world" (*Their Eyes Were Watching God*); the vignettes that Alice Childress penned about the smart, humorous Black woman domestic, Mildred, in *Like One of the Family*; the everyday urban working-class laborers such as Jesse B. Semple ("Simple") and Alberta K. Johnson ("Madam") that Langston Hughes crafted to voice philosophical gems. I was awed by the way Gloria Naylor's *Mama Day* contrasts notions of academic fieldwork with everyday work in fields and the way Jesmyn Ward's *Men We Reaped* chronicles Black men's lives reaped as readily as crops. These are but a few of the many texts by African American authors that address labor, texts that range from the slave narratives, through the Harlem Renaissance, the 1940s and 1950s, the civil rights era, as well as writings from the 1980s to 1990s, through these early years of the twenty-first century.[6] If the literary authors themselves deemed labor an important topic, I felt an urge to continue the legacy of writing about the conflicted situation of those stereotyped as both lazy yet fit for the most menial and arduous labor, those who, nevertheless, understood the dignity and necessity of work. Thus, after I chaired three different departments at Ohio State University (women's studies, English, African American and African studies) and was the senior administrator for two of its academic support units (vice provost for diversity and inclusion and vice president for outreach and engagement), I began to take my scholarship in a different direction, daring to write about the vexed topic of academic labor.

Academic labor is uneasy ground for faculty of color because of the way it has stymied the careers of so many of us. Certainly, service can be a trap, especially when institutions fail to assess its value, when constituents and stakeholders neglect attending to substantive matters, when vision statements are more cosmetic than instructive, and when faculty of color continue to be underrepresented. Although very much aware of the pitfalls of taking on too much service and fully committed to protecting anyone needing such protection, I want to reclaim, reframe, and reimagine service as honorable, honest, fulfilling, and *yes, pleasurable work*. As I argue in an essay for *College English* in which I justify my penchant for rendering service to the academy, even at the cost of no longer formally teaching in the classroom, "There is the administrative pleasure of actually getting things done. It is not nearly the same joy as reading a Toni Morrison novel, nor is it as provocative an experience as discussing the future of the humanities. What high-level administration provides is the opportunity to revise the rules, reclaim what and who has been marginalized, and renegotiate terms of engagement."[7]

Why have I performed in so many different administrative capacities for the academy?[8] My North Star was not to earn tenure and promotion but an internal drive instilled by foremothers and community members long before I learned that I was something called "a first-generation underrepresented student" and long before I knew what such concepts as "liberal education," "shared governance," and "strategic action plans" meant. Whatever service I have given to my university, department, or discipline was not for some promise of upward mobility in the academy. When one serves because one wants heretofore marginalized voices to be heard, one is working for oneself, one's family, and one's community. Or, as politician and preacher Al Sharpton clarified at the Queen of Soul's funeral, Aretha Franklin never "worked" for President Trump as Trump had asserted. On August 31, 2018, in front of the crowd at Detroit's Greater Grace Temple with the nation listening in, Sharpton told Trump: "No, [Aretha] used to *perform* for you. She worked for us."[9] Similarly, I *performed for the academy*; I worked for my family and community, a community whose folklore and literature have much to say about service.[10] There may be multiple layers of reasons as to why one does a particular set of tasks. Oftentimes, onlookers mistake why persons of color do tasks that on the surface seem to be aiding their own subjugation, or, in terms of the academy, jeopardizing their road to tenure. There is this confusion between "performing for" and "working for"—the former a label for what onlookers see and the latter the inner drive that prompts the activity. Some term this double-play as a kind of mask wearing, as voiced by the protagonist in Ralph Ellison's *Invisible Man*:

> I want you to keep up the good fight. I never told you, but our life is a war and I have been a traitor all my born days, a spy in the enemy's country ever since I give up my gun back in the Reconstruction. Live with your head in the lion's mouth. I want you to overcome 'em with yeses, undermine 'em with grins, agree 'em to death and destruction, let 'em swoller you till they vomit or bust wide open.[11]

Notwithstanding that Ellison's protagonist seems engaged in warfare chicanery, the point remains that labor can be calculated, measured, and assessed on a number of different culturally defined registers.

A SERVICE AESTHETIC

Along with a service ethic, I have a service aesthetic. Here I am deeply indebted to scholar Simone Drake's book, *When We Imagine Grace: Black Men and Subject Making*. The phrase "imagining grace" is from Baby Suggs's sermon in the wilderness, or what the novel *Beloved* calls the Clearing. According to Drake, "The Clearing functions as a safe space that affirms blackness. It is a space where Baby Suggs, holy, instructs her congregation of abused, tired, and disenfranchised black people to love themselves because no one else will. Without judgment, Baby Suggs tells them 'that the only grace they could have [is] the grace they could imagine.'" For Drake, "imagining grace" gives agency to Black masculinities, prompting a move away from crisis narratives to an emphasis on the power of self-definition: "imagining grace is an agentic activity that resists stereotypes and homogenous constructions of black masculinity."[12]

Such a move has prompted further thinking on my part. Initially, I agreed to do administrative work because I saw myself serving a community often neglected by the academy, a community rife with practical problems, creating a situation in which I could ill afford to say no. Like Eva in Morrison's *Sula*, I did not want to play "rang-around-the-Rosie" when those important to me metaphorically had only three beets to eat, sores in their mouths, and worms in their bowels—the situation Eva summarizes as: "Pearl was shittin' worms and I was supposed to play rang-around-the-rosie?"[13] In other words, in the past I have argued how senseless it is for faculty of color to ignore or discount the immediate, raw needs of family members and communities who supported their academic journey. How does one say no to requests from the Black Student Union, or to a women's group wanting to address issues of gender and race, or to an international-studies committee that lacks domestic diversity? [14] I always have felt a duty to "represent"—street lingo for the process of standing in for the community. Drake's intervention in the crisis narrative has helped me to realize that much of the diversity service that I have been rendering, like the Black men's lives of which Drake speaks, has been stereotyped, ridiculed, and maligned. But the empowering moment is reclaiming, reframing, and reimagining *the grace of self-hood* that makes it possible to place critical thinking in action, exercising good citizenship that goes beyond the walls of the academy and influences the lives of others. To quote the final words in *When We Imagine Grace*: "But self-love surely is critical to believing one is worthy of grace."[15] My service is important because it completes me. It is at the core of how I choose to circulate within my worlds of influence.

I further note that in Baby Suggs's sermon, Baby Suggs speaks of grace as both a noun and a verb, imploring her community to *grace* all the bodily parts that slavery has harmed—noosed necks, chopped-off hands, lynched bodies, mouths of silent screams, everything from lungs to wombs, from outside parts to inner organs.[16] That is, one takes what has been deemed to be of little value and restores it to its personal and communal value and does so with pride and purpose. Baby Suggs's sermon is included in a chapter that begins by discussing wholeness, Sethe's need to see her sons as "whole in the world because in her dreams she saw only their parts in trees."[17] It is this type of wholeness, of gracing what has been viewed as mundane, tangential, disparate, fragmented work that ultimately drives my passion for service to the academy. There are those who keep working for the greater good, who keep fighting for engaged scholarship, who feel a sense of duty to facilitate the careers of others, who want to reimagine, reframe, and reclaim the value and virtue of service, who want *to grace* service. Gracing service has many practical dimensions, including working with various committees and levels of university administration to ensure that service is truly a respected part of the tenure and promotion process and that effort has been given to assessing and measuring service. Gracing service places service as a core value of any distinguished profile, on par with and often integrated into research and teaching. Gracing service includes doing away with metaphors that describe faculty entering service as traveling into a dark tunnel and reframing such a journey as life sustaining. Gracing service puts into practice the belief that "service is the rent we pay for living."[18]

SERVICE AS A LEGACY:

As someone who is no longer in the classroom, it is my work with students outside the classroom that now returns to me in meaningful ways: the many undergraduate students I took with me to archives who now send me their published work and the former graduate students who do social justice work inside and outside the academy and tell me how I influenced them. In total, I have served on over one hundred MA examinations and theses, general examinations, and PhD dissertation committees. Looking back, I do not regret the many hours I spent listening to an advisee who left her job at a strong research-intensive institution for what she announced was her dream job at a private liberal arts college; or the many calls from an advisee who always seemed to be taking on too many challenges, only to receive her latest call announcing that she is now associate provost and dean of the faculty at her institution; or the calls from the former advisee whose senior professors at his tenure-initiating institution were failing to continue the work of informing him how to transition his scholarship from dissertation to book.

Although all of my graduate advisees who sought tenure-track jobs obtained them, I am equally pleased with the time I spent with those who made other choices: the postdoctoral fellow I groomed for a position teaching literature who recently announced that he has taken a job as a director of an honors program because he has seen how much I enjoyed administration; or one of my top students, a very excellent teacher I mentored for years, who surprised me by saying no to the professoriate and yes to a position as a senior diversity leader. As professors, we cannot always count on the few hours in the classroom that in the long run will make a difference in students' lives. More often, it is the mentoring, patience, and time we give them throughout their lives—the ongoing service—that is priceless. This type of work has not taken away from my career; it has added to it by leaving a legacy of students nationwide who will in turn render service to their communities.

There are also various types of engaged scholarship that academics tradition- ally have dismissed as nothing more than community service. For thirty-two years I served as the executive director of a community reading group, a gath- ering that some would call a book club, but I hesitate to use the latter term because we did not have rules as to who could join or other restrictions. One simply had to have a love of literature and a willingness to probe deeply the selected texts. Initiated by African American women graduates from the first institution where I taught, Denison University, the group approached me requesting that I continue to meet with them to read African American wom- en's literature. I quickly told them that since they were now graduates, they could meet on their own and read whatever they wanted. However, they were seeking the leadership of a professor who would be willing to suggest literature that would challenge their minds and hearts and provoke deep thought and conversation. As someone always ready to answer the question, What book would you recommend I read?, I consented after first reminding the former students that I was now teaching full time at another university, and my time was limited. We selected the name Womanist Readers and met every four to six weeks at someone's home or a local library for the next thirty-two years.

That founding core of Denison graduates invited their friends, mothers, and coworkers to our gatherings. In fact, Janet George, the mother of one of the founding members, served as my assistant director throughout those thirty-two years. As a group, we read hundreds of novels, poetry collections, plays, short stories, and creative nonfiction, mostly about the Black experience. But we also read many other writings by a wide range of authors (e.g., Amy Tan, Barbara Kingsolver, Anita Diamant, Nadine Gordimer, Sandra Cisneros, Louise Erdrich, Lee Martin, J. D. Vance) because the larger goal was always to discover what lit- erature says about the human experience. We convened community workshops on reading Toni Morrison, donated multicultural children's books to local day- care centers, convened special Black History Month read-ins at the Columbus Metropolitan Library, and took group treks to hear Reginald McKnight, John Edgar Wideman, Natasha Trethewey, Jewell Parker Rhodes, Zadie Smith, Tayari Jones, Percival Everett, Randall Kenan, James McBride, Wil Haygood, and many others. Although initially I suggested many of the books, I increasingly trusted group members to suggest readings. Most of them followed my lead, suggesting texts that had depth (my bias, given that I preferred reading only those books that I could teach in my university classroom). Of course, once everyone was offering suggestions and our selections became more elastic and capacious, I braced myself for genres I had had no previous intention of reading, including an interestingly quirky story of a racist white family that adopts a dog only to learn that the dog speaks Black vernacular English.[19]

Learning should always be a two-way street, and my conversations with Womanist Readers on what constitutes literature were as illuminating and contentious as such conversations are in university classrooms. What has been remarkable is this: when my colleagues look at my curriculum vitae details and under "Community Service" see "Executive Director, Womanist Readers," I am sure that their eyes pass over this entry quicker than even the time they give to a book review entry, missing the fact that although people have come and gone from the group, some starting satellite groups in other cities, I have had a "classroom" of many of the same community students for three decades. That is, with Womanist Readers I have had a core group with whom I pretty much started a class, African American Literature 101, and have taken that *same group* to African American literary doctoral studies! The long stint with Womanist Readers has been the one endeavor that has connected me to the pioneer teachers who taught in one-room schools throughout rural America. Often, one teacher taught the same group of students from first through sixth grades. Because of the physical conditions of many of these schools, the teacher arrived early at the humble structure not simply to instruct but to do such tasks as warming up the potbelly stove. With my formal teaching under the quarter system, students passed in and out of my classroom doors quicker than I could learn their names. Although longer, the semester system still did not provide the experience of seeing multiple years of the same students learning before my very eyes, as the aforementioned pioneer teachers were able to do with their students and as I was able to do with the Womanist Readers group. As with the pioneer teachers in those one-room schools who started fires in potbelly stoves, my function at the Womanist Readers gatherings was to fire up the discussion, ignite flames, provide the sparks of information from my background in literature that would warm the room for all the readers to participate in the conversation. Thus, my thirty-two years of service to a community reading group has not been marginal or tangential; it has been the crown jewel of full professorship.

In sum, as a recent retiree, instead of having dreams about running to the wrong classroom at the wrong time as I had done so many years during my teaching career, I find myself wide awake, hilariously watching television's *Judge Judy* (Judith Blum Sheindlin) who tells those who appear before her courtroom all the things that as an administrator I was often tempted to tell colleagues, staff, and board trustees (e.g. "Don't play with me. I have other things to do today"; "If you are trying to second-guess where I'm going, you're not going to be successful"; "I don't care about nonsense. I care about common sense"; "I don't care what you feel. Take your feelings to the Dr. Phil Show"; "How is it that you are here without your evidence? Where did you think you were coming today?—to the beach?"; "Don't put luck and brains in the same category"; "We're done"). Although senior administration has had its low moments, a good sense of humor has mellowed those moments. Indeed, my current watching of *Judge Judy*[20] is a good replacement for the trove of administration cartoons from the *New Yorker* that I kept in my desk drawer all the years when I chaired.

As I look back over a forty-two-year career in higher education, I am appreciative of the teaching and research awards that I have received. However, I am most honored by a recent string of service awards. I stand by the sentiment expressed and words that I crafted with a group of African American women professors and staff for the commemorative collection *This Bridge We Call Home*: there are those of us who, although supportive of the needs of all our colleagues, staff members, and students, have been "invest[ed] heavily in tending the dreamscapes of the marginalized." As with our foremothers, we have sat around kitchen tables discussing service, acts of social justice, and "at the day's end we remain Third World women living in a third space working a third shift. But we have learned that working the third shift has one irrevocable advantage: *we are awake while others sleep, and in that wakefulness, we safeguard dreams.*"[21] Years ago we were, unwittingly, expressing the spirit of what I am now calling "gracing service," a term with reverberations of a high and holy calling.

Again, thanks to the profession for the Francis Andrew March Award, for recognizing, honoring, and yes, *gracing* service.

After receiving the ADE honor, I considered myself fully retired with some minor exceptions—conducting previously scheduled academic program reviews; advising dissertation students already in my pipeline; coediting a book series; delivering diversity lectures; and writing reference letters. I bask in the sunshine of my kitchen and family rooms without paying much attention to what day it is, reclaiming the joy of Sunday evenings, for there are no longer any Monday mornings. There is no longer the rush after watching *60 Minutes* to get lesson plans, clothing outfits, and calendar conflicts sorted out for the ensuing week. I ride around between the times after the school buses have picked up children in the morning and before those same buses return the children home in the afternoon. There is no guilt if I find myself at a store during work hours. As a devout reader who never imagined turning any page except a printed page, I have listened to audible books, thoroughly enjoying hearing Trevor Noah read his autobiography, *Born A Crime,* with his multiple voices. I have even tried to imagine myself a housewife, going as far as to read the newspaper's Sunday morning column, "Hints from Heloise." If ever there are solutions that exceed the nature of the problems, they are in this column: to tightly close a box, cut off the waistband of old pantyhose; save empty dog food bags to use as trash can liners; place dirty diapers in empty bread bags; use white chalk to cover up ring-around-the-collar; place books that have a mildew odor in a freezer for weeks and then place the books in kitty litter containers.

My colleagues have asked me what I do all day, as if there is nothing to do if one is not reading email or attending meetings. My days still go fast with putting together fifteen-hundred- to two-thousand-piece puzzles, decluttering my bedroom and basement, visiting grandchildren, heading educational activities for my church and local community, intentionally getting in ten thousand steps a day, and each night after dinner, there's *Jeopardy* to watch to make sure my brain is still ticking. Some academic duties remain: coediting a university book series, keynoting selected conferences, attending alumni committee meetings, and serving as an external reviewer for tenure and promotion cases. The good part of retirement is that I can be very selective about the life of the mind. One of the pleasures that my own institution has formed is an Emeritus Academy for retirees who have submitted evidence that they are still doing activities that merit grants from the provost's office and who still would like to attend and deliver on-campus lectures. Every lecture that I now attend is because I really want to hear the speaker and not because a dean, provost, or president expects me to be there or because I have to set an example for my colleagues. I sit and listen without texting or looking at my calendar. I have freed myself to be an engaged scholar.

I also have freed myself to concentrate on my next generation of advisees, my own grandchildren. After hearing President Obama and First Lady Michelle read Peter H. Reynolds's book, *The Word Collector* (2018), I instructed my daughter and her husband to purchase that book for their daughter, five-year-old London, my oldest grandchild. London FaceTimed me and started reading the book that describes the different items that people collect: stamps, coins, rocks, art, and so forth. When she turned to the page that discloses that a little boy, Jerome, collects words, London proudly announced, "That's what I want to be when I grow up—a word collector," a wonderful aspiration for her professor of English grandmother to hear. Listening to a grandchild read has reinforced for me why I wanted to retire. I am trying hard for catch-up time with family. My children celebrated my final retirement by coming home for the holidays. We had a family pajama contest on Christmas morning (I will spare readers that picture) but am sharing our on-the-deck picture (see figure 10.1).

Figure 10.1. Christmas at the Lees, December 2019. From left to right: Dr. R. LaMar Cochran holding children, London and Chase Cochran, and wife Dr. Jessica Lee Cochran; Adam Lee; Dr. Valerie Lee and husband, James C. Lee, Esq.; Erica Lee and fiancé, Deshaun Harris, Esq.; Jessica Wilson Lee holding Lucas Christian Lee, and husband Andrew Lee. Courtesy of Phillips Photography & Videography.

Epilogue

When angry, Ma Bell would curse us with the threat, "These trees will see you under." When she told her husband, Grandpop, to build a chicken coop, she wanted the coop to surround Grandpop's favorite tree. Fearful that a coop of chickens would shorten the life of the tree, Grandpop complained. Exasperated that Grandpop could think that trees could be so easily destroyed, Ma Bell predicted, "These trees will see you under." If anyone was in danger of a shortened life, it was Grandpop and not the trees. Ma Bell used the phrase to humble the arrogant and the prideful. Whenever Junebug or Pookie would brag about how they were going to make it in life by scamming or hustling others, Ma Bell would warn, "You better act right. These trees will see you under." When cousin Danika announced that she was "grown and didn't have to obey her momma anymore," Ma Bell shot back, "You think you can do it all, but these trees will see you under."

Years passed before I truly understood what Ma Bell meant by her constant refrain. She was giving us a lesson on mortality. We are here on Earth for a relatively short time compared to the mountains, the rivers, and yes, the trees. She was telling us that we can do whatever we feel we are big enough to do but that we should also realize there is a price to be paid. Ma Bell was saying that one day the large oaks from which we hung our swings, the honeysuckles from which we sipped nectar, and the weeping willows under which we cried for unrequited love would all one day "see us under." Her religious philosophy was to live your life knowing that you have a finite timespan and knowing that the natural landscape would outlive the human body.

Ma Bell's wisdom has helped me bring balance to my life and keeps my ego in check. There are timelines, priorities, responsibilities, and values that I must respect during my brief tenure on this earth. There is no time for haughtiness or evil surmising because "these trees will see me under." In retirement, I have moved on from thinking about hair roots to Ma Bell's tree roots. Dying just shy of 101 years old, Ma Bell was a sequoia.

INTRODUCTION

1 Toni Morrison, *Song of Solomon* (New York: Alfred A. Knopf, 1977), 315.
2 Lucille Clifton, "Homage to My Hair," in *Two-Headed Woman* (Amherst: University of Massachusetts Press, 1980), 5.
3 Tayari Jones, *An American Marriage* (Chapel Hill, NC: Algonquin, 2018), 28.
4 One of the early discussions of the ways that the Aunt Jemima stereotype has informed the relationships between white and Black women is Diane Roberts's *The Myth of Aunt Jemima: Representations of Race and Region* (1994). The history of how Aunt Jemima reflected American racial relationships and the roots of its power as an icon are also traced in M. M. Manring's *Slave in a Box: The Strange Career of Aunt Jemima* (1998). In addition to the many attacks on Quaker Oats' Aunt Jemima icon, there also have been changes to the Black man's picture on Uncle Ben's rice and the Black man's picture on Cream of Wheat cereals. During summer 2020 there were criticisms of and/or changes to other food products because of their racist connotation (e.g., Eskimo Pie, Mrs. Butterworth's syrup). At the end of Summer 2020, Mars Food changed the name of its product, Uncle Ben's rice, to Ben's Original, as the word "uncle," reminiscent of the relationship of masters to male slaves, was part of the problem.
5 Ta-Nehisi Coates, *Between the World and Me* (New York: Spiegel Grau, 2015),10.
6 Morris Beja and Christian K. Zacher, *Not Even Past* (Columbus: Impromptu, 2019), 111. I am honored to be in the company of the two past chairs, Julian Markels and James Phelan.
7 These comments reflect chapter titles from duCille's *Skin Trade*. She titles chapter 4, "Discourse and Dat Course: Postcolonality and Afrocentricity."
8 Morrison, *Sula* (New York: Alfred A. Knopf, 1976), 52.

9   Teresa De Lauretis, *Alice Doesn't: Feminism Semiotics Cinema* (Bloomington: Indiana University Press, 1984), 11.

10 Rebecca Wanzo, *The Content of our Caricature* (New York: New York University Press, 2020), 27.

11 As far back as 2007, I worked with Dolan Hubbard, Paula Krebs, David Laurence, Doug Steward, and Robyn Warhol on a long list of specific actions for departments of English. This list was published in *ADE Bulletin* 141–142 (Winter–Spring, 2007).

12 Randy Pausch with Jeffrey Zaslow, *The Last Lecture* (New York: Hyperion), front flap.

13 *Hamilton: An American Musical*, music and lyrics by Lin-Manuel Miranda, dir. Thomas Kail, chor. Andy Blakenbuehler, Richard Rodgers Theater, New York, NY, February 2, 2016. "The Room Where it Happens" is the fifth song in Act II, and "Who Lives, Who Dies, Who Tells Your Story" is the last song in the performance.

CHAPTER ONE

1   "Yellow wasted" is a folk expression referring to Blacks who do not make "effective use" of their light skin. "Marrying dark" dilutes the advantage of lightness. For a discussion of the politics of this type of "colorism," see Margo Natalie Crawford's analysis of Wallace Thurman's *The Blacker the Berry* in *Dilution Anxiety and the Black Phallus*.

2   Sherley Anne Williams, *Dessa Rose* (New York: Berkeley, 1986), 257.

3   Morrison, *Playing in the Dark* (Cambridge, MA: Harvard University Press, 1992), xii.

4   Morrison, *Tar Baby* (New York: Alfred A. Knopf, 1993), 113.

5   Note that there are two spellings for locks (locs) and two spellings for dread-locks (dreadlocs).

6   Valerie Lee, *Granny Midwives and Black Women Writers* (New York: Routledge, 1996), 38.

7   Dorothy Roberts, *Killing the Black Body* (New York: Pantheon, 1997), 9.

8   Nowlie Rooks, "Wearing Your Race Wrong: Hair, Drama, and a Politics of Representation for African American Women at Play on a Battlefield," in *Recovering the Black Female Body: Self-Representations by African American Women*, ed. Michael Bennett and Vanessa D. Dickerson (New Brunswick, NJ: Rutgers University Press, 2000), 284. For a historical overview of the topic of African American women's hair that pays particular attention to Madame C. J. Walker and the aesthetics of African American women's culture in general see Rooks's book, *Hair Raising: Beauty, Culture, and African American Women* (New Brunswick, NJ: Rutgers University Press, 1998).

9   Initially many of the hairstyles with which African American women experimented were associated with "low-class taste," primarily because young

girls and teenagers were the major wearers of certain styles (e.g., synthetic extension braids). Also, with some styles, such as the Jheri curl, hair strands dripped with water and other products, necessitating the wearing of shower caps, sometimes in public venues. In more recent years, locks/locs have had a special appeal to African American women in academe.

10 For a further discussion of Black women's bodies and hair technologies see Owens Patton's "Hey Girl, Am I More Than My Hair? African American Women and the Struggles with Beauty, Body Image and Hair." *National Women's Studies Association Journal* 18, no. 2 (2006): 24–25.

11 Mariame Kaba, "When Black Hair Tangles with White Power," in *Tenderheaded: A Comb-Bending Collection of Hair Stories*, ed. Juliette Harris and Pamela Johnson (New York: Pocket, 2001), 106.

12 Ayana Byrd and Lori L. Tharps, *Hair Story: Untangling the Roots of Black Hair in America* (New York: St. Martin's Press), 177–78.

13 Ann duCille, *Skin Trade* (Cambridge: MA: Harvard University Press), 82.

14 Carla Peterson explains her use of "eccentric" in *Doers of the Word: African American Women Speakers and Writers in the North (1830–1880)* and in her "Foreword" to *Recovering the Black Female Body: Self-Representations by African American Women*, ed. Michael Bennet and Vanessa D. Dickerson (New Brunswick, NJ: Rutgers University Press, 2000): "I have chosen to term the Black female body 'eccentric,' insisting on its double meaning: the first evokes a circle not concentric with another, an axis not centrally placed (according to the dominant system), whereas the second extends the notion of off-centeredness to suggest freedom of movement stemming from the lack of central control and hence new possibilities of difference conceived as empowering oddness" (See *Recovering the Black Body*, xi, xii).

CHAPTER TWO

1 Adam P. Kennedy and Adrienne Kennedy, *Sleep Deprivation Chamber: A Theatre Piece* (New York: Theatre Communications Group, 1996), 8.

2 "Reckless eyeballing" is a term used to refer to the activity of Black men who desire white women, a behavior considered irresponsible given what could be fatal consequences, such as lynching. Because Emmett Till dared to look and whistle at or speak to a white woman, he was guilty of "reckless eyeballing." In 1986 Ishmael Reed popularized the term in his satirical novel, *Reckless Eyeballing*.

3 This is the statement that Mamie Till, Emmett Till's mother, made at his funeral. She deliberately held an open-casket funeral as a witness to "what they did to my boy."

4 Toni Morrison, *Song of Solomon* (New York: Alfred A. Knopf, 1977), 81.

5 Bebe Moore Campbell, *Your Blues Ain't Like Mine* (New York: G. P. Putnam's Sons, 1992), 65.

6   Gwendolyn Brooks, *The World of Gwendolyn Brook* (New York: Harper & Row, 1971), 323.

7   Kennedy and Kennedy, *Sleep Deprivation Chamber*, 6.

8   Cornel West, *Race Matters* (Boston: Beacon, 1993), xii.

9   West, *Race Matters*, xiii

10 Henry Louis Gates, *Loose Canons: Notes on the Culture Wars* (New York: Oxford University Press, 1992), 37, 38.

11 Randall, Dudley. *The Black Poets* (New York: Bantam, 1971), 121–122.

12 Kennedy and Kennedy, *Sleep Deprivation Chamber*, 8.

13 Kennedy and Kennedy, 16.

14 Founded by leading civil rights attorneys, Peter Neufeld and Barry Scheck, the Innocence Project is responsible for most of the postconviction DNA exonerations in the United States. The book has photographs of and interviews with 124 persons. Neufeld and Schneck are associated with the Benjamin N. Cardozo School of Law in New York City. Taryn Simon is the photographer and interviewer for the book project.

15 Taryn Simon, Paul Neufeld, and Barry Scheck, *The Innocents* (New York: Umbrage Editions, 2003), 28. This is a book of photographs and interviews by Taryn Simon.

16 Simon, Neufeld, and Scheck, *The Innocents*, 28.

17 Simon, Neufeld, and Scheck, 28.

18 Houston Baker Jr., *Turning South Again* (Durham, NC: Duke University Press, 2001), 2–3.

19 Toni Morrison, *Birth of a Nation'hood* (New York: Pantheon, 1997), xxi.

20 Baker, *Turning South Again*, 6, 7.

21 Williams, *Alchemy of Race and Rights*, 234.

22 Kennedy and Kennedy, *Sleep Deprivation Chamber*, 33.

23 A version of these letters appeared in two blogs I wrote for my university soon after the incidents took place: https://buckeyevoices.osu.edu/articles/2014/12/18/a-letter-to-my-twin-sons/); https://buckeyevoices.osu.edu/articles/2014/01/09/madiba's-lessons/.

CHAPTER THREE

1   The book jacket for *Last Chance for the Tarzan Holler* says that "the holler of the title (and of the title poem) is born when the sentient being—man, woman, or child—grapples with mortality at the last moment: at the moment before baptism or, for Susan Smith's sons strapped in their car seats, just before the lake waters close over them. It's a last burst of vivacity, a holler that affirms and resists the very demise that it heralds."

2   Valerie Lee, *Granny Midwives and Black Women Writers* (New York: Routledge), 6, 24, 88.

3　Katherine Clark tells Onnie Lee Logan's story in *Motherwit: An Alabama Midwife's Story*. (New York: E. P. Dutton), 1989.

4　Lee, *Granny Midwives*, 12–14.

5　Karla Holloway. *Moorings and Metaphors: Figures of Culture and Gender in Black Women's Literature* (New Brunswick, NJ: Rutgers University Press, 1992), 522

6　Lee, *Granny Midwives*, 3.

7　See Layli Phillips and Barbara McCaskill's discussion of Black women in academic settings in "Who's Schooling Who? Black Women and the Bringing of the Everyday into Academe, or Why We Started *The Womanist*," *Signs* (Summer, 1995): 1008–10.

8　Jessica Care Moore, "There Are No Asylums for the Real Crazy Women" in *The Words Don't Fit in My Mouth* (New York: Moone Black, 1997), 38–39.

9　Marlon T. Riggs, "Unleash the Queen," in *Black Popular Culture*, ed. Gina Dent (Seattle: Bay, 1992), 102.

10　In *Black Writers of America*, ed. Richard Barksdale and Keneth Kinnamon (New York: Macmillan, 1972). This folktale is called "Swapping Dreams." See pp. 230–31. Because of the oral tradition, there are many variations of the same stories; see, for example, the folktales in *Mother Wit from the Laughing Barrel*, ed. Alan Dundes (Englewood Cliffs, NJ: Prentice-Hall, 1973); *A Treasury of Afro-American Folklore*, ed. Harold Courlander (New York: Crown, 1976); *Shuckin' and Jivin'*, Daryl Cumber Dance, ed. (Bloomington: Indiana University Press, 1978); *Afro-American Folktales: Stories from Black Traditions in the New World*, ed. Roger D Abrahams (New York: Pantheon, 1985); *Talk That Talk: An Anthology of African-American Storytelling*, ed. Linda Goss and Marian E. Barnes (New York: Simon & Schuster, 1989); *Call and Response: The Riverside Anthology of the African American Literary Tradition*, ed. Patricia Liggins Hill (Boston: Houghton Mifflin, 1998); *From My People: 400 Years of African American Folklore*, ed. Daryl Cumber Dance (New York: W.W. Norton, 2002),

11　Amy Hill Hearth interviewed the Delaney sister and helped them write *Having Our Say* (New York: Dell, 1993). The sisters were known for their wit and gifted oral history storytelling.

12　I heard Willie Gary tell this story at a banquet in Columbus, Ohio, in the mid-1990s.

13　Ralph Ellison, *Invisible Man* (New York: Random House, 1952), 107.

14　Langston Hughes, *The Best of Simple* (New York: Hill and Wang, 1961), 60–61.

15　Toni Cade Bambara, *Gorilla, My Love* (New York: Random House, 1972), 88.

16　Bambara, *Gorilla, My Love*, 89.

17　Bambara, 94.

18　Bambara, 89.

19　Gloria Naylor, *Mama Day* (New York: Ticknor and Fields, 1988), 7.

20 Toni Morrison, *Beloved* (New York: Alfred A. Knopf, 1987), 251.

21 Robin D. G. Kelley, *Yo' Mama's Disfunktional!* (Boston: Beacon, 1997), 1–13.

22 Alice Walker, "Everyday Use," in *In Love & Trouble* (New York: Harcourt Brace Jovanovich, 1973), 57.

CHAPTER FOUR

1 Ruth Frankenberg, *White Women, Race Matters: The Social Construction of Whiteness* (Minneapolis: University of Minnesota Press, 1993), 6.

2 Ian F. Haney Lopez, *White By Law: The Legal Construction of Race* (New York: New York University Press, 1996), 18.

3 Matt Wray and Annalee Newitz, eds., *White Trash: Race and Class in America* (New York: Routledge, 1997), 4.

4 This advisee, who has given me permission to print his entrance essay to our program, finished his PhD studies, accepted a tenure-track position, and after a few years became the director of an honors program at a state university. He is a diversity advocate and remains an avid reader of Black women's texts.

5 Most of the comments were either too frank, too dismissive, or too revealing of the students' identities for me to include. I have tried to be discreet with the ones I quote.

6 Leslie Marmon Silko, *Ceremony* (New York: Viking/Penguin, 1977), 2, 3. The six-stanza poem that begins *Ceremony* uses two voices—what "he said" and "what she said."

7 See Joy Harjo, *How We Became Human: New and Selected Poems: 1975–2001* (New York: W.W. Norton, 2002). As the back jacket of this collection notes, Harjo is "known for her signature blend of storytelling, prayer, and song." My assumption is that to be human is to tell a story.

8 Randall Kenan in *Free Within Ourselves: Fiction Lessons for Black Authors*, ed. Jewell Parker Rhodes (New York: Doubleday, 1999), 293.

9 Teresa De Lauretis, "Semiotics and Experience," in *Alice Doesn't: Feminism, Semiotics, Cinema* (Bloomington: Indiana University Press), 984.

10 Joan Scott, "Experience," *Critical Inquiry* 17, no. 4 (Summer 1991), 779.

11 Margaret Walker, "Street Demonstration," in *The Black Poets*, ed. Dudley Randall (New York: Bantam, 1971), 156.

12 Ann duCille, *Skin Trade* (Cambridge, MA: Harvard University Press, 1996), 1.

13 At the time of this writing, Frank W. Hale Jr. was vice provost and special consultant to the president emeritus of Ohio State University. He has written several books on diversity and was a former president of historically Black Oakwood University.

14 This is a common tenet of critical white studies. For example, in critiquing Bakke's assumption as to his failure to be selected to the medical school at the University of California (Davis), critical white theorist Vada Berger writes: "Every accomplishment [whites] would like to claim as their own is tainted by

having been gained through their whiteness. Therefore, the truly questionable group in any medical school setting, the ones who should operate in a 'cloud of suspected incompetency,' are the white students." Quoted in *Critical White Studies: Looking Behind the Mirror*, eds. Richard Delgado and Jean Stefancic (Philadelphia: Temple University Press, 1997), 110.

15 Baldwin's notable quotes can be found on several sites. See https://www.goodreads.com/quotes.

16 Angelou's s notable quotes can be found on several sites. See https://www.goalcast.com/2007/04/03/maya-angelou-quotes-to-inspire-your-life/.

17 duCille, *Skin Trade*, 83.

18 Toni Cade Bambara, "What It Is I Think I'm Doing Anyhow," in *The Writer on Her Work*, ed. Janet Sternburg (New York: W.W. Norton, 1980), 165.

19 Morrison mentions this metaphor in an interview with Nellie McKay. See *Contemporary Literature* 24, no. 4 (1983): 413; see also *Conversations with Toni Morrison*, ed. Danille Taylor-Guthrie (Jackson: University Press of Mississippi, 1994), 138.

CHAPTER FIVE

1 I am indebted to Professors Jared Gardner and Sebastian Knowles for crafting the workload plan.

2 These phrases can be found in many of the speeches of Shirley Chisholm (1972 Democratic Convention) and Marian Wright Edelman. See Edelman, *The Measure of Our Success: A Letter to My Children and Yours* (New York: HarperCollins, 1993).

3 Valerie Lee, "Smarts: A Cautionary Tale," in *Calling Cards: Theory and Practice in the Study of Race, Gender, and Culture*, ed. Jacqueline Jones Royster and Ann Marie Mann Simpkins (Albany: State University of New York Press, 2005), 104.

4 There is no monolithic Black community. Here I am speaking of the community as it has been spoken of and romanticized in Black churches, community centers, folklore, and African American literature. My point is that however debatable these notions may be, they have had an effect on many of the African Americans who assume professional jobs whether in the academy, law firms, or corporations.

5 Jerald Walker, "Visible Man," *Chronicle of Higher Education*, October 12, 2007. C2–C3.

6 Walker, "Visible Man," C3.

7 April L. Few, Fred P. Piercy, and Andrew Stremmel, "Balancing the Passion for Activism and the Demands of Tenure: One Professional's Story from Three Perspectives," *NWSA Journal* 19, no. 3 (Fall 2007): 47–66.

8 Few, Piercy, and Stremmel, "Balancing Passion," 49–58.

9 Few, Piercy, and Stremmel, 62.

10 Few, Piercy, and Stremmel, 62.

11 This particular variation is told in Richard Barksdale and Keneth Kinnamon, eds., *Black Writers of America: A Comprehensive Anthology* (New York: Macmillan, 1972), 457.

12 The historical connection between mules and African American women is best summarized by Nanny in Zora Neale Hurston's *Their Eyes Were Watching God* (Urbana: University of Illinois Press, 1978), 29. "De nigger woman is de mule uh de world so fur as Ah can see. Ah been prayin' fuh it tuh be different wid you. Lawd, Lawd, Lawd!"

13 Zora Neale Hurston, "Sweat," in *Sweat: Zora Neale Hurston*, ed. and intro. Cheryl A. Wall (New Brunswick, NJ: Rutgers University Press, 1997), 28.

14 John Lowe, "*From Jump at the Sun: Zora Neale Hurston's Cosmic Comedy*" in *Sweat: Zora Neale Hurston*, ed. and intro. Cheryl A. Wall (New Brunswick, NJ: Rutgers University Press, 1997), 184.

15 Alice Childress, *Like One of the Family: Conversations from a Domestic's Life* (Boston: Beacon, 1956; rpt. 1986), 119–122.

16 Toni Morrison, *Sula* (New York: Alfred A. Knopf, 1976), 68.

17 Morrison, 68.

18 Morrison, 69.

19 Morrison, 69.

20 Gwendolyn Brooks, "Kitchenette Building," in *Selected Poems* (New York: Harper & Row, 1963), 3.

21 Gwendolyn Brooks, "First Fight. Then Fiddle," in *Selected Poems* (New York: Harper & Row, 1963), 54.

22 See "Affirmative Activism: Report of the ADE Ad Hoc Committee on the Status of African American Faculty Members in English, "*ADE Bulletin* 141–142 (Winter–Spring 2007), 70–74. In this essay the team of Dolan Hubbard (Morgan State University), Paula Krebs (Wheaton College), David Laurence (ADE), Valerie Lee (Ohio State University), Doug Steward (ADE), and Robyn Warhol (University of Vermont) looks at some alarming statistics, such as "of the approximately 400 institutions that have graduated African American undergraduates who have gone on to complete a PhD in English, 192 produced only one in the past thirty-three years" (p. 70). The essay outlines a number of strategies to address a range of issues faced by African American graduate students, undergraduate students, and faculty.

23 The Summer Institute for Literary and Cultural Studies (SILCS) is a four-week institute at Wheaton College that targets students from ethnic or racial groups who are underrepresented in the field of English studies.

24 The Program for Arts and Humanities Development (PHD) is a two-year research and mentoring program that targets students from historically underrepresented groups, focusing on providing summer classes, mentoring, and year-long financial support for graduate work in the arts and humanities.

25 The Summer Research Opportunities Program (SROP) is an initiative spon-
sored by the Big Ten Alliance Academic universities, formerly the Committee
on Institutional Cooperation (CIC) that targets underrepresented students. For more information, see their website at https://www.btaa.org/
resources-for/students/srop

26 Few, Percy, and Stremmel, "Balancing Passion," 58.

27 Alice Walker, *Her Blue Body Everything We Know: Calling Earthling Poems
1965–1990* (San Diego, CA: Harcourt Brace Jovanovich, 1991), 160.

28 Marilyn Mobley McKenzie, "Labor Above and Beyond the Call: A Black
Woman Scholar in the Academy," in *Sister Circle: Black Women and* Work, ed.
Sharon Harley and the Black Women and Work Collective (New Brunswick,
NJ: Rutgers University Press, 2002), 243. As Mobley McKenzie mentions in
her essay, there is a long history of racial uplift formally dating back to the
motto of the National Association of Colored Women, "Lifting as We Climb."
As I was finishing my own essay, I read Mobley McKenzie's essay. Had I not
been so busy with academic service and read it earlier, I would not have felt
a need to write my piece. Her story resonates with my story. That is, we are
senior professors looking back on our careers—a very different posture from
the young professor that I quote at the beginning of my essay.

29 McKenzie, "Labor Above and Beyond," 241.

30 "Andrea's Third Shift: The Invisible Work of African American Women in
Higher Education" in *This Bridge We Call Home*, ed. Anzaldua and Keating
(New York: Routledge), 403.

31 In Esther 4:14, Mordecai, representing his community, warns Esther: "For if
thou altogether holdest thy peace at this time, then shall there enlargement
and deliverance arise to the Jews from another place; but thou and thy father's
house shall be destroyed: and who knoweth whether thou art come to the
kingdom for such a time as this?"

32 McKenzie, "Labor Above and Beyond," 237.

33 Gloria Naylor, *Mama Day* (New York: Ticknor and Fields, 1988), 7.

34 Alice Walker, "Everyday Use," in *In Love and Trouble* (New York: Harcourt
Brace Jovanovich, 1973), 57.

CHAPTER SIX

1 Octavia E. Butler, *Kindred*, intro. Robert Crossley (Boston: Beacon, 2003) ix.

2 William Andrews, *To Tell a Free Story: The First Century of the African-
American Autobiography, 1760–1865.* (Urbana: University of Illinois
Press,1986), 14.

3 Bernard W. Bell, *The Afro-American Novel and its Tradition* (Amherst:
University of Massachusetts Press, 1987), 289.

4 See Ashraf H. A. Rushdy's *Neo-Slave Narratives: Studies in the Social Logic
of a Literary Form* (New York: Oxford University Press, 1999), 3. This is one

of the early discussions of what Rushdy calls "the contemporary narrativity of slavery." Rushdy focuses his study on William Styron's *Confessions of Nat Turner*, Ishmael Reed's *Flight to Canada*, Sherley Anne Williams's *Dessa Rose*, and two works by Charles Johnson, *Oxherding Tale* and *Middle Passage*. Throughout his book, Rushdy makes a case for a connection between the neo-slave narratives and a specific set of political issues of the 1960s.

5 Charles T. Davis and Henry Louis Gates Jr., *The Slave's Narrative* (New York: Oxford University Press, 1985), xv, xvi.

6 Linda Brent, *Incidents in the Life of a Slave Girl*, intro. Walter Teller (New York: Harcourt Brace Jovanovich, 1973), 79.

7 This quote is from the book cover of *Whiteness: A Critical Reader*, ed. Mike Hall (New York: New York University Press, 1997).

8 Toni Morrison, *Playing in the Dark: Whiteness and the Literary Imagination* (Cambridge, MA: Harvard University Press 1992), xii.

9 Elizabeth Ellsworth in *Off White: Readings on Race, Power, and Society*, ed. Michelle Fine et al. (New York: Routledge 1997), 264.

10 For a discussion of "The New Abolitionists" see Noel Ignatiev's article in *Transition: An International Review* 73 (1991), 199–203. Ignatiev addresses his fellow white citizens to become new abolitionists, and to do so "they must commit suicide as whites to come alive as workers or youth or women or artists or whatever other identity will let them stop being the miserable, petulant, subordinated creatures they now are and become freely associated, developing human beings" (200). Ignatiev also speaks of the new abolitionism in *Race Traitor*, the collection he coedited with John Garvey. Winner of the 1997 American Book Award, *Race Traitor* argues: "When we speak of the new abolitionism, we mean something other than the stances normally taken under the banner of 'anti-racism.' We mean a challenge to the institutions that reproduce race as a social category—a challenge that disrupts their normal operation." See Noel Ignatiev, *Race Traitor* (New York: Routledge, 1996), 3.

11 Sherley Anne Williams, *Dessa Rose* (New York: Berkeley), 39.

12 Deborah McDowell, *Slavery and the Literary* Imagination. (Baltimore: Johns Hopkins University Press, 1989), 146.

13 Toni Morrison, *Beloved* (New York: Alfred A. Knopf, 1987), 251.

14 George Lipsitz, *The Possessive Investment in Whiteness: How White People Profit from Identity Politics* (Philadelphia: Temple University Press, 1998), vii.

15 James Baldwin, "On Being White ... and Other Lies" quoted in *James Baldwin: The Cross of Redemption, Uncollected Writings*, ed. Randall Kenan (New York: Pantheon, 2010), 136.

16 Cheryl I. Harris, "Whiteness as Property," in *Critical Race Theory: The Key Writings That Formed the Movement*, ed. Kimberlé Crenshaw et al. (New York: New Press, 1995), 279.

17 George Lipsitz, *Possessive Investment*, viii.

18 John Suggs, *Whispered Consolations: Law and Narrative in African American Life,* (Ann Arbor: University of Michigan Press, 2000), 12.

19 Williams, *Dessa Rose*, 189.

20 Morrison, *Beloved*, 190.

21 Frederick Douglass writes this in a letter to Wendell Phillips, Esq. of Boston on April 22, 1845. The letter is included with many editions of *Narrative of the Life of Frederick Douglass: An American Slave Written by Himself.*

22 I would argue that Morrison's character Stamp Paid in *Beloved* is a good case example of reparations. With Stamp Paid, Morrison raises questions about when debts are settled. With Clarence Thomas, she raises the issue of how the rescued often are so appreciative as to not want reparations but a chance to keep paying the debt. In her Clarence Thomas/Anita Hill essay, "Introduction: Friday on the Potomac," Morrison argues that "being rescued into an adversarial culture can carry a huge debt. The debt one feels one owes to the rescuer can be paid, simply, honorably, in lifetime service" (xxvii).

23 Suggs, *Whispered Consolations*, 8.

24 Thomas Ross, *Just Stories: How the Law Embodies Racism and Bias,* (Boston: Beacon, 1996), 23, 24.

25 Richard Delgado, *Critical Race Theory: The Cutting Edge* (Philadelphia: Temple University Press, 2000), xiv.

26 Patricia Williams, *The Alchemy of Race and Rights* (Cambridge, MA: Harvard University Press, 1991), 7, 8.

27 Butler, *Kindred*, 9.

28 Rushdy, *Neo-Slave Narratives*, 7.

29 This is critic Trudier Harris's simile and can be found in her review essay of *Beloved*.

CHAPTER SEVEN

1 Johnson v. Lovett in *Judicial Cases Concerning American Slavery and the Negro*, ed. Helen Tunnicliff Catterall, vol. 3 (Buffalo: William S. Hein & Co.), 78–79. All of this chapter's nineteenth-century legal cases are from the five volumes of *Judicial Cases*.

2 Catterall, *Judicial Cases*, 5:4.

3 Catterall, 3:676.

4 Catterall, 5:158.

5 William Andrews, *To Tell a Free Story: The First Century of the African-American Autobiography, 1760–1865* (Urbana: University of Illinois Press, 1986), 14.

6 Ralph Ellison, *Invisible Man* (New York: Random House, 1952), 137.

CHAPTER EIGHT

1 Stan Hunt, "Employer to Employee," Condé Nast Collection, *New Yorker*, January 7, 1980.

2   Warren Miller, "A Man Rows a Boat by Himself," *New Yorker Collection*, the Cartoon Bank, May 28, 1990.

3   Barbara Smaller, Image ID: TCB-46557, *New Yorker Collection*, the Cartoon Bank, May 11, 2001.

4   Charles W. Mills, *The Racial Contract* (Ithaca, NY: Cornell University Press, 1997), 11.

5   Mills, *Racial Contract*, 40.

6   One of the most prominent cartoons in the category of animals expounding on diversity is "A Fish at a Dog Bar Says" by Charles Barsotti, In the cartoon three dogs are drinking, and the dog bartender, upon looking at the fish, says, "I'm Going to Have to See Some Identification." (See https//condenaststore.com/collections/Charles+Barsotti?page=2). My favorite fur-bearing animal cartoon I clipped from an issue of the *Chronicle of Higher Education*'s "Letters to the Editor" section. Illustrated by David Williams, the fur-bearing animal, sitting at the head of a table with four senior-looking white men sitting on the side of the table, leans forward and says, "You know, I'm the only fur-bearing animal on the committee, and I'm getting damned suspicious."

7   Charles Barsotti, "Rattlesnake Boss Rattles His Tail at an Employee," *New Yorker*, October 13, 2003.

8   This cartoon by Peter Steiner appears in *The Complete Cartoons of the New Yorker*, edited by Robert Mankoff with a foreword by David Remnick (New York: Black Dog & Leventhal), 618.

9   This cartoon by Robert Mankoff appears in *The Complete Cartoons of the New Yorker*, edited by Robert Mankoff with a foreword by David Remnick (New York: Black Dog & Leventhal), 487.

10 Joy Harjo, "The Power of Never," in *How We Became Human: New and Selected Poems: 1975–2001* (New York: W.W. Norton, 2002), 143.

11 Recent scholarship on Black cartoonist Jackie Ormes includes Kelly Jo Fulkerson-Dikuua's essay, "Refashioning Political Cartoons: Comics of Jackie Ormes, 1938–1958" in *Are You Enter-Tained?*, ed. Simone C. Drake and Dwan K. Henderson (Durham, NC: Duke University Press, 2020), 101–117.

12 During the summer of 2020, prior to publication of *Sisterlocking Discoarse*, I had the opportunity to talk to Angelia Lee about her cartoons.

13 See chapter 4, "'What Did TSA Find in Solange's Fro'? Security Theater at the Airport," 131–159. Browne discusses the disproportionate number of bodily searches of Black women and a number of national and international airport stories about violated Black bodies.

CHAPTER NINE

1   I first shared these reflections as a one-page personal essay in 1991 for the Denison University Alumni magazine.

2 Toni Morrison dedicates *Beloved* to "*Sixty Million or more.*" See her interview with Walter Clemons for her explanation: Walter Clemons, "A Gravestone of Memories," *Newsweek*, September 28, 1987, 74–75.

3 Alan Behr, "The Quiet Island" (Tribune News Service), *Columbus Dispatch*, August 30, 2015.

4 During the time of Mandela's death, I first shared a version of my visit to South Africa in a blog post : https://buckeyevoices.osu.edu/articles/2014/01/09/madiba's-lessons/.

5 Philip Kennicott, "A Monument to Pain" *Columbus Dispatch*, April 27, 2018.

6 Michele Norris. *The Grace of Silence: A Memoir* (New York: Pantheon, 2010), xiv.

CHAPTER TEN

1 Kathryn Stockett, *The Help* (New York: G.P. Putnam's Sons, 2009), 443.

2 Although very smart, my mother had only a high school education.

3 My husband is an attorney, and although helpful, he could not always juggle his court dates.

4 Toni Cade Bambara, "What It Is I Think I'm Doing Anyhow," in *The Writer on Her Work*, ed. Janet Sternburg (New York: W.W. Norton, 1980), 165.

5 Although many Black feminists speak of wholeness in terms of "both/and" rather than unnecessary divisions, these specific references are from an essay by Toni Cade Bambara on what she was attempting to accomplish in her novel *The Salt Eaters.*

6 To make this point, this essay cites some of those essays.

7 Valerie Lee, "Symposium: How I Have Changed My Mind," *College English: Celebrating the NCTE Centennial Symposium* 74, no. 2 (November 2011): 120.

8 For a fuller discussion of why I performed administrative work, see "Pearl was shittin' worms and I was supposed to play rang-around-the-rosie?" in *Over Ten Million Served: Gendered Service in Language and Literature Workplaces.*

9 Videos of Sharpton's speech are easily accessed online.

10 See "Smarts: A Cautionary Tale" in *Calling Cards: Theory and Practice in the Study of Race, Gender, and Culture.* In this essay I argue that African American folklore and literature foreground issues of communities' understandings of work and labor.

11 Ralph Ellison, *Invisible Man* (New York: Random House, 1952), 161.

12 Simone Drake, *When We Imagine Grace: Black Men and Subject Making* (Chicago: University of Chicago Press, 2016), xiii, 2.

13 Toni Morrison, *Sula* (New York: Alfred A. Knopf, 1976), 69.

14 See the original wording of this position in Valerie Lee, "Pearl was shittin' worms."

15 Drake, *When We Imagine Grace*, 209.

16 Toni Morrison, *Beloved* (New York: Alfred A. Knopf, 1987), 88.

17 Morrison, *Beloved*, 86.

18 The popular quote, "Service is the rent we pay for living," and variations thereof, have been attributed to several African American leaders, most notably Shirley Chisholm and Marian Wright Edelman.

19 The story is "Black Betty" by Nisi Shawl who writes speculative fiction.

20 I am not unaware of some of the problematics of Judge Judy's courtroom. A comprehensive critical analysis of the program can be found in Ann duCille's *Technicolored: Reflections on Race in the Time of TV* (2018) where duCille critiques Judge Judy's handling of specific race and class issues, noting that Judge Judy extends "mercy to dogs and distraught dog owners" (216) but has little time or patience for "browbeaten, belittled loser litigants" (220).

21 Toni C. King et al., "Andrea's Third Shift: The Invisible Work of African-American Women in Higher Education," in *This Bridge We Call Home*, ed. Gloria E. Anzaldua and Analouise Keating (New York: Routledge, 2002), 414.

Allen, Theodore. *The Invention of the White Race.* Vol.1: *Racial Oppression and Social Control.* Verso: London, 1994.

Anzaldúa, Gloria E., and Analouise Keating, eds. *This Bridge We Call Home: Radical Visions for Transformation.* New York: Routledge, 2002.

Baker, Houston, Jr. *Turning South Again: Re-Thinking Modernism/Re-Reading Booker T. Washington.* Durham, NC: Duke University Press, 2001.

Bambara, Toni Cade. *Gorilla, My Love.* New York: Random House, 1972.

_____. "What It Is I Think I'm Doing Anyhow." In *The Writer on Her Work*, edited by Janet Sternburg, 153–68. New York: W.W. Norton, 1980.

Beja, Morris, and Christian K. Zacher. *Not Even Past: A History of the Department of English. The Ohio State University, 1870–2000.* Columbus, OH: Impromptu, 2019.

Brodkin, Karen. *How Jews Became White Folks and What That Says About Race in America.* New Brunswick, NJ: Rutgers University Press, 1998.

Brooks, Gwendolyn. *The World of Gwendolyn Brooks.* New York: Harper & Row, 1971.

Browne, Simone. *Dark Matters: On the Surveillance of Blackness.* Durham, NC: Duke University Press, 2015.

Byrd, Ayana D., and Lori L. Tharps. *Hair Story: Untangling the Roots of Black Hair in America.* New York: St. Martin's Press, 2001.

Campbell, Bebe Moore. *Your Blues Ain't Like Mine.* New York: G.P. Putnam's Sons, 1992.

Catterall, Helen Tunnicliff, ed. *Judicial Cases Concerning American Slavery and the Negro.* 5 vols. Buffalo, NY: William S. Hein, 1998.

Clifton, Lucille. *Two-Headed Woman*. Amherst: University of Massachusetts Press, 1980.

Coates, Ta-Nehisi. *Between the World and Me*. New York: Spiegel Grau, 2015.

Delgado, Richard, and Jean Stefancic, eds. *Critical White Studies: Looking Behind the Mirror*. Philadelphia: Temple University Press, 1997.

Dent, Gina, and Michele Wallace. *Black Popular Culture,* Seattle: Bay, 1992.

Drake, Simone C., and Dwan K. Henderson, eds. *Are You Enter-Tained? Black Popular Culture in the Twenty-First Century*. Durham, NC: Duke University Press, 2020.

Drake, Simone C. *When We Imagine Grace: Black Men and Subject Making*. Chicago: University of Chicago Press, 2016.

duCille, Ann. *Skin Trade*. Cambridge, MA: Harvard University Press, 1996.

_____. *Technicolored: Reflections on Race in the Time of TV*. Durham, NC: Duke University Press, 2018.

Ellison, Ralph. *Invisible Man*. New York: Random House, 1952.

Fine, Michelle, and Lois Weis, Linda C. Powell, and L. Mun Wong. *Off White: Readings on Race, Power, and Society*. New York: Routledge, 1997.

Frankenberg, Ruth. *The Social Construction of Whiteness: White Women, Race Matters:* Minneapolis: University of Minnesota Press, 1993.

Gates, Henry Louis, Jr. *Loose Canons: Notes on the Culture Wars*. New York: Oxford University Press, 1992.

Harris, Cheryl I. "Whiteness as Property." In *Critical Race Theory: The Key Writings That Formed the Movement,* edited by Kimberlé Crenshaw, Neil Gotanda, Gary Peller, and Kendall Thomas, 279. New York: New Press, 1995.

Harris, Juliette, and Pamela Johnson, eds. *Tenderheaded: A Comb-Bending Collection of Hair Stories*. New York: Pocket, 2001.

Holloway, Karla. *Moorings and Metaphors: Figures of Culture and Gender in Black Women's Literature*. New Brunswick, NJ: Rutgers University Press, 1992.

Hubbard, Dolan, Paula Krebs, David Laurence, Valerie Lee, Doug Steward, and Robyn Warhol. "Affirmative Activism: Report of the ADE Ad Hoc Committee on the Status of African American Faculty Members in English." *ADE Bulletin*, no. 141–142 (Winter–Spring, 2007): 70–74.

Hughes, Langston. *The Best of Simple*. New York: Hill and Wang, 1961.

Ignatiev, Noel. *How the Irish Became White*. New York: Routledge, 1995.

Jones, Tayari. *An American Marriage*. Chapel Hill, NC: Algonquin, 2018.

Kalanithi, Paul. *When Breath Becomes Air*. New York: Random House, 2016.

Kennedy, Adam P., and Adrienne Kennedy. *Sleep Deprivation Chamber: A Theatre Piece*. New York: Theatre Communications Group, 1996.

Kelley, Robin, D. G. *Yo' Mama's Disfunktional! Fighting the Culture Wars in Urban America*. Boston: Beacon, 1997.

King, Toni, Lenora Barnes-Wright, Nancy E. Gibson, Lakesia D. Johnson, Valerie Lee, Betty M. Lovelace, Sonya Turner, and Durene I. Wheeler.

"Andrea's Third Shift: The Invisible Work of African-American Women in Higher Education." In *This Bridge We Call Home: Radical Visions for Transformation*, edited by Gloria E. Anzaldúa and Analouise Keating, 403–15. New York: Routledge, 2002.

Lee, Valerie. *Granny Midwives and Black Women Writers: Double-Dutched Readings*. New York: Routledge, 1996.

———. "Symposium: How I Have Changed My Mind." *College English: Celebrating the NCTE Centennial Symposium* 74, no. 2 (November 2011): 118–20.

Lipsitz, George. *The Possessive Investment in Whiteness: How White People Profit from Identity Politics*. Philadelphia: Temple University Press, 1998.

López, Ian F. Haney. *White by Law: The Legal Construction of Race*. New York: New York University Press, 1996.

Mankoff, Robert, ed. *The Complete Cartoons of the New Yorker*. New York: Black Dog & Leventhal, 2004.

Manring, M. M. *Slave in a Box: The Strange Career of Aunt Jemima*. Charlottesville: University Press of Virginia, 1998.

Morrison, Toni. *Beloved*. New York: Alfred A. Knopf, 1987.

———."The Official Story: Dead Man Golfing." In *Birth of a Nation'hood: Gaze, Script, and Spectacle in the O.J. Simpson Case,* edited by Toni Morrison and Claudia Brodsky Lacour, vii–xxviii. New York: Pantheon, 1997.

———. *Playing in the Dark: Whiteness and the Literary Imagination*. Cambridge, MA: Harvard University Press, 1992.

———. *Song of Solomon*. New York: Alfred A. Knopf, 1977.

———. *Sula*. New York: Alfred A. Knopf, 1976.

———. *Tar Baby*. New York: Alfred A. Knopf, 1993.

Moss, Thylias. *Last Chance for the Tarzan Holler*. New York: Persea, 1998.

Naylor, Gloria. *Mama Day*. New York: Ticknor and Fields, 1988.

Pausch, Randy, with Jeffrey Zaslow. *The Last Lecture*. New York: Hyperion, 2008.

Roberts, Diane. *The Myth of Aunt Jemima: Representations of Race and Region*. New York: Routledge, 1994.

Roberts, Dorothy. *Killing the Black Body: Race, Reproduction, and the Meaning of Liberty*. New York: Pantheon, 1997.

Rooks, Noliwe. M. *Hair Raising: Beauty, Culture, and African American Women*. New Brunswick, NJ: Rutgers University Press, 1996.

Shange, Ntozake. *Nappy Edges*. New York: St. Martin's Press, 1978.

Stockett, Kathryn. *The Help*. New York: G. P. Putnam's Sons, 2009.

Suggs, Jon-Christian. W*hispered Consolations: Law and Narrative in African American Life*: Ann Arbor: University of Michigan Press, 2000.

Walker, Alice. *The Color Purple*. New York: Harcourt Brace Jovanovich, 1982.

———. "Everyday Use." *In Love &Trouble*. New York: Harcourt Brace Jovanovich, 1973.

Wanzo, Rebecca. *The Content of Our Caricature: African American Comic Art and Political Belonging*. New York: New York University Press, 2020.

West, Cornel. *Race Matters*. Boston: Beacon, 1993.

Williams, Patricia J. *The Alchemy of Race and Rights: Diary of a Law Professor*. Cambridge, MA: Harvard University Press, 1991.

Williams, Sherley Anne. *Dessa Rose*. New York: Berkeley, 1986.

Wray, Matt, and Annalee Newitz, eds. *White Trash: Race and Class in America*. New York: Routledge, 1997.

ritual, at airports, 112; locks/locs, 24, 142–43n9; low-class taste, 142–43n9; natural hair, 2–3, 23, 25; professionalism, 27; "sisterlocks," 23; weaponizing of, at airports, 112–13; white definitions of professionalism, 25–26

Black women's studies, 24. *See also* African American women's studies

Bland, Sandra, 5

Boyce-Taylor, Cheryl, 6

Brazil, 118–19

Brooks, Gwendolyn: "First Fight, then Fiddle," 72–73; "kitchenette building," 72; "Last Quatrain of the Ballad of Emmett Till, The," 31; "To Those of My Sisters Who Kept Their Naturals," 2

Brooks, Rayshard, 5

Brown v. Board of Education, 71

Brown, Elsa Barkley: quilting of history, 41–42

Browne, Simone: *Dark Matters: On the Surveillance of Blackness*, 112–13

Brown, H. Rap, 53–54

Brown, John, 87

Brown, Michael, 5, 37

Brussels (Belgium), 6, 119

Burke, Tarana, 8

Butler, Octavia: *Kindred*, 10, 14–15, 77–78; slave narratives, stretching boundaries of, 86

Byrd, Ayana D., 3

Calvert County (Maryland), 53–55

Campbell, Bebe Moore: *Your Blues Ain't Like Mine*, 30–31

Cape Town (South Africa), 121–22

Caribbean, 15, 118, 120–21

cartoons, 101, 106, 136; animals, 15, 104; animals, and diversity, 103, 152n6; Black women, 15, 107; and diversity, 103–4; as gendered, 104–5; patriarchal influence, satirizing of, 102–3; as raced, 104–5; white men and affirmative action, satirizing of, 103

Carver, George Washington, 99

Chicago (Illinois), 119

Childress, Alice: *Like One of the Family: Conversations from a Domestic's Life*, 71, 129

Chisholm, Shirley, 67, 154n18

chokehold, 7

Chronicle of Higher Education (journal), 15, 101, 152n6

Cisneros, Sandra, 134

civil rights movement, 123, 130

Cliff, Michelle, 14; *Free Enterprise*, 78

Clifton, Lucille: "Homage to My Hair," 2

Coates, Ta-Nehisi, 7

Colbert, Cynthia: "The Kink That Winked," 3

colonialism, 120

Color Purple, The (film), 105

Color Purple, The (Walker), 55–57

colorism, 118; marrying dark, 142n1; yellow wasted, 142n1

Confederacy, 6, 123

Congo, 6, 119

conjure women: double-headed, 41; double wisdom, 41; sistah conjurers, 41

Conrad, Joseph: *Heart of Darkness*, 115

Cooper, J. California, 14; *Family*, 78, 86

Cosby Show, The (television series), 106

COVID-19, 8; "Lost Summer," 4; as public health crisis, 5

crack: and powdered cocaine, 62

Crawford, John, 37

Cream of Wheat, 141n4

Crenshaw, Kimberlé, 77

critical race feminism, 79, 85–86

critical race studies: slave narratives, 15

critical race theory, 77, 79, 84–85; legal concepts, subverting traditional definitions of, 82; and property, 82

critical white studies, 146–47n14

Critical White Studies (Delgado), 84

Crossley, Robert, 77–78

Cullen, Countee: "What Is Africa to Me?" 115

Davis, Frank Marshall: "Robert Whitmore," 32

Notorious B.I.G., 43

Oakwood University, 93, 146n13; slave cemetery, 94–95, 97, 99
Obama, Barack, 119, 138
Obama, Michelle, 105, 138
Off White (Fine), 84
Ohio State University, 130, 146n13; academic service, 65; African American faculty, 66–68; Department of English, 63–65, 66, 102; Department of History, 63–64; Department of Women's Studies, 66; Department of Women's Studies, newsletter column, 22; Diversity Action Plan, 60; Diversity Council, 59–61, 74; Graduate and Professional Day program, 62; meritocracy, 66–67; patriarchy, 66; as PWI (predominantly white institution), 100; redistribution of teaching and service expectations plan, 66–67; University Compensation Committee for Faculty Governance, 74; white privilege, 66; workload plan, 65–66
Ormes, Jackie, 107
Other, 117–18
overrepresented people, 104
Owens, Jesse, 54

patriarchy, 66
Pausch, Randy: *Last Lecture, The*, 16
Perkins-Valdez, Dolen, 15; *Wench*, 78
Peter Blow plantation, 95
Peterson, Carla L., 25, 143n14; "Eccentric Bodies," 17
Phelan, James, 141n6
Plessy v. Ferguson, 85
Pretoria (South Africa): "Wall of Names," 121
Prince Frederick (Maryland), 53

Quaker Oats: Aunt Jemima mascot, 6, 141n4

race, 13, 18–19, 22, 40, 44, 49, 55, 74, 76, 79, 84–85, 87; and beauty, 17; Black nationalists, 120; and gender, 16, 23, 25, 63, 104, 117–18, 120–21, 132; as metaphor,

for people of color, 32; as narrative of property, 82; as social construction, 52; as sociopolitical category, 32
racial profiling, 47
racial reckoning, 6
racial uplift, 149n28
racism, 46, 82, 118; systemic racism, as public health crisis, 5; as visceral experience, 7
Reading in the Wilderness Student Association, 107
reckless eyeballing, 143n2
Reed, Dorothy, 25
Reed, Ishmael, 15; *Flight to Canada*, 78; *Reckless Eyeballing*, 143n2
reparations, 151n22
reverse discrimination, 62
Reynolds, Peter H.: *Word Collector, The*, 138
Rhodes, Jewell Parker, 134
Rice, Tamir, 5, 37
Riggs, Marlon: "Unleash the Queen," 44
Robben Island, 123
Roberts, Dorothy: *Killing the Black Body*, 24
Robeson, Paul, 71
Robinson, Anthony, 33–34
Rooks, Noliwe M., 3, 24
"Room Where It Happens, The" (song), 142n13
Roper, Moses, 79
Ross, Thomas, 84–85
Rushdy, Ashraf: *Neo-Slave Narratives*, 86–87

Salvador (Brazil), 119
Selma (Alabama), 7
Scheck, Barry, 144n14
school integration, 53
Scott, Dred, 94–95
Scott, Joan, 59
self-hood: grace of, 132
Selma (film), 105
sexism, 118
Shange, Ntozake: *For Colored Girls who considered Suicide when the Rainbow is Enuf*, 10; *Nappy Edges*, 2